FILL THE GAP

HOW TO MANIFEST FROM WHERE YOU ARE NOW TO THE LIFE YOU WANT

TASHAI LOVINGTON

TARAZOD
PRESS

For more by Tashai Lovington, go to her website at:

https://tashai.net

Cover design: © 2022 by Tashai J Lovington

Copyright 2022 by Tarazod Press LLC

ISBN: 9798986194707 (softcover)

ISBN: 9798986194714 (ebook)

PRAISE FOR TASHAI LOVINGTON

"I think a lot of people need to take advantage of this. I'm thrilled that you are doing the work, because it's so needed."
- **Jack Canfield,** New York Times Best Selling Author of *The Success Principles* and Co-creator of the #1 Best Selling book series *Chicken Soup for the Soul*

∾

"Tashai is so encouraging and inspires you to live a better life!"
—**James Malinchak**, featured on ABC's Hit TV show, "Secret Millionaire", Founder, www.BigMoneySpeaker.com

∾

"Tashai Lovington has mastered the art of engagement by capturing the reader's attention from the first page all the way through to the end. She has taken her own life experiences and her astute observations and skillfully incorporated them into insightful spiritual life lessons. Her book, Fill the Gap offers universal principles and wisdom to the neophyte as well as the seasoned life student which is much needed in the world today. Kudos to the author and I recommend that you pick up a copy of Fill the Gap now!"
—**Sue Corbin,** Author, Speaker, & Trainer

MOTIVATE AND INSPIRE OTHERS!

"Share this Book"

special quantity discounts

QUANTITY	PRICE
5-20 books	15.99
21-99 books	14.99
100-499 books	13.99
500-999 books	11.99
1,000+ books	9.99

To place an order contact:
https://tashai.net

THE IDEAL PROFESSIONAL SPEAKER FOR YOUR NEXT EVENT

Any organization that wants to develop their people to become "extraordinary," needs to hire Tashai for a keynote and/or workshop training!

TO CONTACT OR BOOK TASHAI TO SPEAK:
Tashai Arts LLC
6516 Monona Dr.
Suite 311
Monona, WI 53716
https://tashai.net

THE IDEAL COACH FOR YOU!

If you're ready to overcome challenges, have major breakthroughs and achieve higher levels, than you will love having Tashai as your coach!

TO CONTACT OR BOOK TASHAI TO SPEAK:
Tashai Arts LLC
6516 Monona Dr. Suite 311
Monona, WI 53716
https://tashai.net

Thanks to Robert,
for being on this path with me.

CONTENTS

INTRODUCTION

We are physical beings. It's a material world. This is not news; we have five senses which tell us this on a daily basis. And yet, let's establish here at the outset, we are also more than this. Much more, in fact. A broader part of us exists. It is alive and well at this very moment—in the non-physical.

It doesn't matter what we call this aspect of ourselves. The name isn't important, connecting with it in a real way is. Higher self, true self, inner self, inner being, soul, the source, the force, the universe, or God. A label is a label. However, if you want to effect real change in your life, to finally make the money, find the lover, or get healthy again, then you're going to also want to enhance your awareness of this aspect of yourself, that is, to come into sync or vibrational resonance with it.

What you will learn in this book is not a luxury. It's a necessity. Why? Because you are investing in yourself. While everything else may fall away, your knowledge and self-development is yours forever. And with these, who you really are will always continue to expand and unfold.

This book is for you, the individual who has tried self transformation but it just hasn't been as life-changing as you thought it would be. Or it seems to only work intermittently. You have not yet found your success. If this sounds like you, I will help you fill that gap from where you are now to where you want to be.

If you are serious about changing your life, this book will give you the tool kit to manifest the success that has always alluded you. No matter what your focus, be it financial abundance, improved personal relationships, better health or anything else, you can achieve your goals. Think of it like this, you are standing on the edge of a canyon and before you is a deep wide gorge. The success you desire is on the other side, but it feels insurmountable. This book is your bridge. Within are the tools to get you to that other side.

Effort and struggle are not a prerequisite for manifesting the life you want. Using simple but effective techniques, you can open yourself to the true power of focused intent.

I think it's important to note here that I'm not more special than you. I don't have all the answers. I'm not a guru or a perfect spiritual teacher. I've just been on this path for quite some time, and through life experience and exposure to other teachers and mentors, I've learned a number of things along the way. Universal principles are not difficult to understand. Their beauty is in the simplicity.

Yet, there is a tendency on our part to overthink and complicate matters. I will lead you through this rocky terrain because I've done it. You want a better life. Let me help you build the bridge to get you there.

Breathe. Let go. And remind yourself that this very
moment is the only one you know you have for sure.
— Oprah Winfrey

ONE

BEGINNINGS

It's never too late to become who you want to be. I hope you live a life that you're proud of, and if you find that you're not, I hope you have the strength to start over.

—F. Scott Fitzgerald

The beginning of one thing is born from the ending of another.

As a kid, I was reasonably adept at following my intuitive guidance. Being an only child, I was left on my own quite often. My father was attempting to finish his PhD. My mother was either working or she was sick and had to go for treatments at the hospital. I often wished I'd had siblings to play with, but this alone time did foster a sense of self-reliance and helped me cultivate a strong connection with my inner voice.

My father's idea of babysitting was to bring me along to the university where he would do whatever research he was working on. I would sit alone in his office, reading or playing with my spirograph. This was before social media, smartphones, or even cable TV. All I had were my books, my drawings, and my own imagination. Occasionally my father took me to visit the animals in another part of the building, but this was rather rare.

Time passed and my mother's cancer went into remission. When she started working again, home life became volatile. It was a rare day when my parents weren't enraged, fighting, and screaming at each other. In the apartment, the car, in public, it didn't matter.

I remember one argument in a city park. My father was always interested in anything with a historical flavor to it. There was a military transport airplane on display and we were going to tour it. Something set them off, however, and I remember my mother dragging me around the outside of the plane as we either ran from or chased after my father— as they screamed at the top of their lungs. I was mortified, not for the first or last time either.

Then one day the fighting became physically violent and my mother left the house in an ambulance. My father was immediately sorry. I could see it in his face. But the damage was done. Soon after, my parents divorced. I was 10 years old.

People started declaring how sorry they were for me because of the divorce. Aunts, uncles, friends of the family, even people I didn't know seemed to think this would devastate me. I tried to explain that the divorce was the best thing that could have happened. My home life was so much more tranquil with my parents not living under the same roof. Yet, when I would say this as a child, nobody believed me, that I could be happy and even celebrate my parents divorce. They thought I was in shock, denial, or in need of counseling. A 10-year-old couldn't possibly differentiate what was best for herself. Bullshit. I knew.

I was home alone a lot after school and still didn't have anyone to talk to. There wasn't much I wanted to watch on television, and the internet wasn't a thing yet. So I learned to be okay with being quiet. And while it wasn't all that great at times—I felt lonely and wished I had someone to play with—it did allow me, as I mentioned earlier, to stay connected to the subtle guidance coming from my inner voice.

There have been many occasions when I discounted my gut instinct and regretted it. Those instances of doubt where I ignored what felt right usually came when I was trying to please other people. Or it was when I was too afraid to take a leap of faith. If I had had the tool set that I'm going to share with you in this book, a lot of unpleasantness could have been avoided. I understand now that the ups and downs in life don't have to be long lasting. That's true for all of us. We are not being tested, but we are growing. Everyday we refine what we want, whether we're consciously aware of it or not.

When I was in my teens, my mother utterly embraced the New Age movement of the 1980s and 90s. Yoga, meditation, breathwork, energy work, crystals, channeling, past lives, all the hot topics of the era. She felt drawn to it, and as a result, so was I. *A Course in Miracles* was her subject matter of choice, but there were many, many others, including Shirley MacLaine's books, the Edgar Cayce material, Richard Bach, and so on. She introduced me to the work of Joseph Campbell, and it was through the power of his words—his books, audios, and videos—that I had discovered my first mentor.

As much as my mother and I were into new thought, you might think we would have met others who shared the same passion. This was not the case, however. My father was an ultra-intellectual, unwilling to even consider the possibility of things beyond our physical existence. My extended family couldn't be bothered either. The few friends we had didn't have a clue what all this oddball stuff was about. Out of fear of being ostracized, my mother kept her fringe beliefs to herself. And by example, I learned to hide mine as well. So on this journey of exploration, it was just mom and me.

While her interest in metaphysical concepts didn't come into focus until the movement became popular in the 1980s, years earlier, an event occurred that would color the rest of her life. In her late teens or early twenties, my mother had a near-death experience. She left her body and entered a beautiful etheric place brimming with love. It permeated her spirit. *A much better place than here,* she would say. However, the angelic-like beings that met her communicated that it wasn't her time. She would need to return to the physical. This incident obviously left a lasting impression on my mother, but not in the positive way you might think. It wasn't that she doubted the continuation of life. She tasted it firsthand so she knew it was genuine. Rather, the issue was one of rejection. To her, it felt like she had gotten the boot from the Garden of Eden. As a result, she never believed that the *heavenly-feeling* she encountered in her NDE could ever be experienced here on earth.

We would share our epiphanies and revelations, discuss our dreams, read some of the same books, and feel a sense of camaraderie—but as I mentioned, only with each other.

Our beliefs we still kept just between the two of us. Fearful of ridicule by family and friends, I learned from my mother to conceal my questions, experiences, or anything else relating to esoteric topics. For most of my life, I hid my deep interest in metaphysical subjects.

Nonetheless, I continued my personal and private journey. I branched out and studied the work of many other teachers. Cultural norms were changing and the mainstream popularity of such authors as Wayne Dyer, Louise Hay, Deepak Chopra and others was signaling a shift in mass consciousness. I devoured their books and other media. I would go to hear them speak when they came to town on book tours or for seminars.

While my friends and extended family remained unaware of my interests, I did eventually feel safe enough to share them with Robert, a college boyfriend (and now my husband). He was open to these ideas too, mainly because his mother practiced automatic writing, and he grew up listening to her read from the Edgar Cayce books, the Seth material, and more.

I wasn't doing myself any favors by hiding this aspect of who I was from the world. But the fearful dialog inside my head insisted that I was keeping safe in this suppression—when just the opposite was true. My life wasn't working, at least not all of the time. For what felt like half of the time. Half of my life wasn't working, not as I knew it could. I did have a wonderful boyfriend, I enjoyed my free time, and had fun with my pets. My jobs, though, were wildly unfulfilling, money was always scarce, and the majority of the hours in my days were spent denying my true self. I would connect up with my inner guidance when playing in the yard with my chickens, while creating art, traveling on vacation, or going to movies with friends. Yet, I would just as easily loose touch watching the clock at whatever dull job I had at the time. I was allowing outside conditions to dictate my emotional state. What I didn't know then was how you feel is a choice, and it's yours to make, no matter what shit may be swirling around you.

I'd like to say that I finally just made a conscious decision to take full responsibility for my life, to embrace this inner part of myself, and that things really began to turn around. I'd like to say this, but it wasn't quite what happened. In reality, there isn't just one single turning point in your life; there are many. I didn't just make up my mind, and suddenly the seas parted. It's been a journey. Step-by-step, choosing to go in the direction of what feels best each and everyday. It's in the *consistency* that you will shine.

My mother's story is a cautionary tale. She endured a great deal of anguish as a child, including poverty, as well as both physical and mental abuse. Sadly, she never transcended the memories of this pain. And unfortunately, that's where many people find themselves, ensnared in the past. My mother died having reached none of the material goals of which she spoke so often, such as owning her own house, being an author, traveling, and retiring wealthy—or at least middle class. It's not that happiness comes from possessions, but in the kind of life she desired, these things would have simply been a natural extension. It never materialized for her.

Why? What happened? Was there something she could have done differently? Somewhere along the line, my mother latched onto the idea that in order to move forward with her life, she first needed to go back. In some circles, this school of thought asserts that you must process and clear old traumas from your psyche if you want to be happy and whole in the present. This is exactly what she hoped to accomplish. She literally refused to do anything toward attaining her future goals until she first wiped clean her troubling past. I remember her talking about catharsis and how good it would be once she was healed of her emotional scars.

Her life became increasingly bleak as she continued to delve into the dark recesses of her anguished youth, only to uncover more painful events and circumstances. One of the definitions of catharsis is *the elimination of a complex by bringing it to consciousness and affording it expression.* A potential problem with this kind of thinking is, as Abraham-Hicks points out, "There is no bottom." The more you go to that place, the more you will activate the vibration of those circumstances.

For some, this exercise of releasing old wounds does bring a certain level of success. Finding and de-activating old thought patterns that no longer serve you is a wonderful and life-force-freeing process. Though, it's also a razor's edge. Jumping headlong into the pit of despair with a pick-and-shovel is not recommended. If you continue to dig around in that stuff, you will only end up attracting more of the same, similar painful feelings that are reflected back in your everyday life. That's the law of attraction. We'll talk more about it in detail in later chapters. For now, just know that a balance must be struck between shining a light on old beliefs verses forging a new path forward for yourself. I'll share several techniques for accomplishing this also in later chapters. First, let's see what happened in my mother's life example.

Dig up your old pain in order to release it. She so believed in this school of thought that she focused on little else. In reality, all she was doing was retraumatizing herself. Her life was only getting worse, and I could see it happening right before my eyes.

After several years of this, I'd honestly had had enough. I staged an intervention, of sorts, and told her point blank that, in my opinion, attempting to clear old emotional scars by fixating on them is not the way to heal your life. I said, *What you focus on only increases and intensifies.* She actually agreed with me but still insisted that what she needed to do first was wipe her past before she could move forward with anything else.

As much as we may want to help others, it's not our place to live someone else's life for them. Even if we don't agree with their choices, it doesn't make us right and them wrong. I tried to talk with my mother about looking in a new direction. I spoke my piece, then told her that, of course, she could do whatever she felt she needed to do. I didn't agree with her actions, but I wouldn't interfere anymore either.

She quit her nursing job which she was really good at but never enjoyed. That was one of the gifts my mother had, she was a fantastic nurturer. With her newfound free time, she spent her days and weeks partaking in sessions with a traditional therapist, writing in journals, and processing all the negative aspects of her life. A few more years passed with no visible improvement in her situation. Then her money ran out. She was forced to take a job filing papers at a car dealership. It was a horrible fit for her, which only made her feel even worse about herself. It wasn't long before cancer had returned to her body.

Right before she got sick, my husband and I were living in a one bedroom apartment in Colorado. We had a small business with another outside partner that was coming to an end. As a result, we were experiencing some financial difficulty. We were considering a move to another state when I received the news about my moms illness. So a decision was made to relocate back to the midwest to be closer to her.

With a sick parent, a business breakup, and a cross-country move, I was suddenly feeling three major life stresses coming at me all at once.

My mother would end up in a nursing home where she would pass a couple years later. Several family members told me how sorry they were that she had lost her lifelong battle with cancer. I know they meant well, but this surprised me in several ways. First because of how it was said, actually in a slightly condescending way. Odd I know, yet it was almost as if they were implying she had failed for not beating the disease.

The *lifelong battle* thing also caught me off guard because she didn't have cancer her entire life. There were two distinct bouts separated by almost 30 years of good health in between. Did people really perceive her as being afflicted her entire adult life? Battling away? This was a revelation to me. She was battling, but it wasn't with cancer. How must they have spoken to her then? Did she let that affect her self-esteem? Many times, it's the well-meaning people around us that offer the most challenges when we are looking to change our lives for the better.

This juncture in my life would become a major dark night of the soul. I stopped any self-improvement I was doing and swore off any new thought principles. My reasoning was, *I've had some amazing experiences, but this stuff really hasn't helped improve the quality of my existence. Life is still a struggle. And look what it did for my mom.* My physical health was suffering, I started loosing my hair, and we were drowning in a sea of debt. I wasn't happy.

In hindsight, I know the issue was similar to my mother's. I simply had stopped listening to my inner guidance and instead was focusing on the aspects of my life that I didn't like. But it took me a while to figure this out.

One thing I actually did continue to do throughout this whole stage of my life was to read the *Notes from the Universe* created by Mike Dooley. I'd been receiving these daily email inspirational messages almost since he first began sending them in the late 1990s. These little nuggets of vibrational truth would eventually help me, once again, to reconnect with my inner voice.

During the next couple of years, I became aware of my body's adverse reaction to grains. Cutting them out of my diet helped improve my health greatly. I devoured information on nutrition and healthy living. I started a quiet daily practice of yoga, and also began exercising, becoming the fittest I had ever been. My interests expanded. I co-produced with Robert a documentary film on keeping backyard chickens in the city, I explored my fascination with ancient cultures and civilizations, and nurtured my love of pet reptiles.

As my focus shifted away from the sad or frustrating baggage in my life and back towards things that inspired my interest, I began to allow my soulful side to trickle back to me a little at a time. My true being was starting to emerge. And on those occasions when I would actually pay attention and follow the impulses that came to me, fun synchronicities were the result. If I was looking for something or had a question, the answers would show up. So I made a vow to start allowing my intuition to guide my life as often as I could.

At the 10 year anniversary of my mother's passing, I

went through the rest of her things that I'd kept. A strange epiphany hit me, my mother got exactly what she wanted.

Always, her biggest underlying desire was, as she put it, *to cross back over to the other side*. It was a yearning she'd felt for the greater part of her life, way more attractive than owning a house or having lots of money. She once told me the only reason she didn't leave the world earlier was because she couldn't abandon me when I was a child. Thanks Mom. She also said she could never end her own life and believed instead that she had to remain here until she was, in her words, *taken back*. Of this, I was obviously grateful too.

Staying in the physical world was, in her mind, a punishment, not a second chance to do something different. She wasn't going to deliberately end her own life, but her illness finally provided the means. The law of attraction brought my mother exactly what she wanted, a return to non-physical. This was a huge revelation for me.

For the first time since her death, I was able to look at her belongings and not feel any blame or anger towards her, at myself or at the mindset that encouraged her to dig up the pain from her past.

The principles of the universe are unerring. You get what your focus on whether you're aware of it or not. Yet, I had been carrying around a ball of wadded-up resistance energy. I was angry at my mother for how her life turned out, and I was angry at myself for the direction mine appeared to be heading. But now, with the realization that my mother had attracted what she actually wanted, something finally released in me.

I felt like I was whole again, like some part of my spirit that I had forsaken, was returning in big way. It was an energetic rush, and I could now be myself again. I had a clearer understanding about what it meant to be here on Earth, and I could start filling in, rather than widening, the gap that stood between me and the life I wanted.

With this new insight, I was able to find forgiveness for her, for things I was holding against her but wasn't even aware of. I forgave her for leaving me too soon, for not being smart about her money, for not following my advise on stopping the negative focus. And I forgave myself too for being so angry at her.

As I go forward, new gaps do appear, but I now have the tools to navigate them. I tend to this everyday, and I will show you how to do the same.

TAKEAWAYS - CHAPTER 1

BEGINNINGS

1. You have an inner being that provides you with guidance
2. You attract the vibrational equivalent of what you focus on

TWO

THE GAP

WHAT IS THE GAP? Basically, it's the discrepancy between the vibration you are currently resonating with and the one you would have if you were living the life of your dreams, one with an amazing romantic relationship or smashingly good health or loads of money flowing to you or whatever it is you desire. What you want is to raise your vibration to this next level, and then the next, and soon the sky is the limit.

If you have not yet achieved the goals that you desire, it doesn't mean that other people who have are somehow better, harder working, or more spiritual than you. It's simply an indication that their degree of expectation in these areas is different than yours. Everyone has things they would like to level up in their life. The more you are connected with your true-self energy, the greater the unfolding. Once a current desire is achieved, new more expanded aspirations are formed, leading to an ever-evolving life for you and also those around you. And since we all have a larger part of us that is non-physical and eternal, we will never be done learning, growing, or advancing.

Sometimes the gap is modest, one where you're already in close proximity to the vibrational frequency of what you want to achieve. It's as if you simply need to walk through a doorway and bam! You've arrived.

We've all had successes in our lives where things have come easily and effortlessly. A parking space opens up for you right in front of the store you're visiting. You find a ten dollar bill on the sidewalk. The phone rings and it's the person you were just thinking about. These seemingly small occurrences are every bit as important as those you might think of as more desirable or substantial, e.g., a new car, a home, a lover. When it comes to manifesting, there is no such thing as too big or too small. The dynamics of manifestation work the same no matter what you focus on, and in theory, they should each come to you with the same amount of ease and fluidity. If they aren't, if you find that manifesting a million dollars is more difficult than one hundred, the issue is not with the subject matter. It's your belief. If you believe it is harder—or impossible—to make a million, then you are manifesting *that* reality with your belief.

It's only the aware person who stops to acknowledge

the little moments of apparent serendipity. Whether you consider something to be minor or monumental, if you celebrate each manifestation, you are giving attention to your good fortune, focusing on the positive rather than the negative. This in turn can only attract more of the same. In doing so, your belief expands beyond where it was before, and a momentum starts to build. And it's this movement forward that will make it possible for you to reach your more ambitious goals.

So if you have a desire that is calling to you, but it seems unattainable, then start with something easier, more in vibrational sync with where your beliefs are currently residing. If it feels too ambitious and you just don't see how it would ever be possible to reach it, that's your gap.

Sometimes the distance between where we are and where we want to be seems so large and daunting that we doubt we can make the jump. It feels like this chasm can't be crossed in one great bound; it's too far and you will fall. Maybe you've even tried and failed before, and now you are left clinging to the side of the canyon wall with one word on your mind. "HOW?"

It's okay. Just because you may not be ready to take a giant leap, doesn't mean you can't get to the other side. Start where you are. Take a few steps in the direction you want to go. Acknowledge the good you've already attracted to you. Build on this. Any step forward is better than none at all and each will get you closer to your destination. In the next chapters I'll explain the techniques you can use to help you actually fill the gap.

TAKEAWAYS - CHAPTER 2

THE GAP

1. The gap is the discrepancy between where you are now and where you want to be
2. No matter how insurmountable it seems, the gap is bridgeable
3. Acknowledge the good fortune you've already attracted into your life

THREE

YOU CAN'T CONTINUE TO FOCUS ON SOMETHING YOU DON'T LIKE AND GET WHAT YOU WANT

SUCCESSFUL PEOPLE MAINTAIN A POSITIVE FOCUS IN LIFE NO MATTER WHAT IS GOING ON AROUND THEM. THEY STAY FOCUSED ON THEIR PAST SUCCESSES RATHER THAN THEIR PAST FAILURES, AND ON THE NEXT ACTION STEPS THEY NEED TO TAKE TO GET THEM CLOSER TO THE FULFILLMENT OF THEIR GOALS RATHER THAN ALL THE OTHER DISTRACTIONS THAT LIFE PRESENTS TO THEM.

—JACK CANFIELD

THE COMMON IDIOM ASKS, *What type are you, a glass half empty or a glass half full?* We've all heard the various positive thinking phraseologies espoused by self-help gurus and social media influencers: *look on the bright side, just keep smiling, only happy vibes.* To some, this may seem like nothing more than pop culture fluff. Yet at its core, this type of messaging is actually aligned with who we really are.

Our non-physical selves are only focused on our greater good. This is played out here in our flesh and blood world through the very real principle of universal magnetics, otherwise known as the law of attraction.

You're probably aware of the idea behind the law of attraction, right? What we focus on expands and like attracts like. Simple really. It draws to us that which is equal to our vibrational frequency. And our natural vibration is one of freedom, joy, love. It's only when thoughts arise contrary to this that we experience things we may label as undesirable. Our thoughts and feelings are what attract the people, places, and things of life.

Everything is a form of energy. Some is physical, some is non-physical. But on a molecular level, it's all energy. Energy vibrates. And it's your thoughts—or more specifically, how your thoughts make you feel—that dictate the speed at which you will be vibrating. Joyful thoughts and emotions vibrate at a certain frequency. Pessimistic thoughts at another.

Okay, but how do I actually practice this law of attraction? Good news! You don't have to. It's already at work everyday whether you know it or not. Your life is shaped from the things you attract. What you can practice is focusing— focusing your attention—in order to get what you want, not just what you are unconsciously reacting to. You can easily test this.

Focus Intention Game

If your intention is free from contradictory thoughts, then what you focus on will show up in your life. It truly is not any more complicated than that. So have some fun. Pick a neutral subject, one that doesn't elicit any negative emotion. If you live in an area, say, with lots of automobile traffic, casually think of a particular make and model of vehicle. Think of it for at least a minute. Then let those thoughts go. Head out about your day as you usually would, but pay attention because soon you'll start seeing this vehicle more and more—and not just today but in the subsequent days to come too.

Enjoyable game. But what does this principle mean in regards to your life? You are the creator of it. The law of attraction serves you. So are you consciously and persistently implementing it? Direction and consistency are the keys. Have a direction and consistently align with it, both mentally and emotionally. These are the things that propel your desires forward, ever expanding and transforming your life to reflect that which you focus on.

On a vibrational level, everyone receives what they put out. We control our own vibration, either unconsciously or through deliberate choice. In a world of media drama, instant feedback, and social causes on all points along the spectrum of life, it's easy to get caught up in issues. This is what trips most people up. The universe does not distinguish. If you key in on injustice in the world, you attract more of the same. You can't continue to focus on something you don't like and get what you want. However, if your center of attention is on people living in harmony with each other, harmony will be in your vibration and will thus be drawn to you.

You don't even have to be that specific. Life already knows what you want. You want to feel good. So any good-feeling emotion or thought, no matter what the subject, will work to raise your frequency and attract more of the circumstances you want that bring you joy. Just pick anything that makes you feel good to be your focal point. This will attract the other things you want as well.

Selective Attention

How do you hone your focus? For now I'd like you to practice *selective attention*. Get your nose out of everyone else's business, and flow your attention only in the direction of the things that make you feel good. Does this mean that you can't have a cause or social crusade? No. It does mean, however, that you will want to direct your focus towards things you are *for* rather than *against* conditions you dislike.

Instead of being against war, be for people acting with tolerance and understanding. Instead of being against hunger, be for everyone having enough to eat. Have your passion projects, but make sure you are really attracting what you prefer. Don't be fooled and inadvertently give energy to what you don't want. No matter the situation, what you focus on is what arrives at your doorstep. The universe (i.e. your subconscious) does not distinguish. Can you tell this is important?

Skeptics often look for the one extreme case where the law of attraction can't possibly be at work. For instance, one might say, *I've been asking for a million dollars forever! I definitely want it. I've been reciting positive affirmations and visualizing it on my dream board. So where is it?* I would respond, *Take a look at what you are really focusing on. Are you truly feeling what it would be like to have a million bucks? Or maybe, without even realizing it, is your attention on the lack of money, how desperately you need it, or how difficult it would be for you to actually manifest it?* The universe knows what you're really harmonizing with, even if you don't.

What if there's a situation where the negativity you're witnessing from someone or something is just so big and in your face that you're unable to find any positive aspect in the situation? Attempting to *not* think about it seems impossible, and in fact, only perpetuates the adversity in your mind's eye. Depending on the situation, you may even feel it's irresponsible not to pay attention to it.

If you find yourself in such a difficult situation, just do the best you can in the moment, and don't beat yourself up if you're unable to maintain a high vibe focus. Life happens. What's important is that you try again later. Whatever you find vibrational harmony with will expand in your life. The more consistent your frequency, the more dominant the manifestation.

It's true, you can't not think a troublesome thought. But you can gently turn your focus in another direction, to another topic altogether, towards something that unfailingly brings you joy. This could be a happy memory, a current event, or future daydream. Lightly nudge your attention away from the troubling circumstance by shifting it towards subjects which bring you warm emotional reactions. This is selective attention.

Direction and Consistency

If you direct your thoughts to things that bring you happiness, and do this on a regular basis—direction and consistency—you will in short order begin to see and feel differently. And when you do, your life will change for the better. As with almost anything, it gets easier with practice. If you fall back, don't get down on yourself. It's part of life.

The goal is not to maintain a negative-free mindset 100% of the time. Instead, you are simply creating an energetic flow in the direction you want your life to go. And the results will be amazing!

In your daily life, for example, let's say the exit ramp you normally take to get to your grocery store is unexpectedly closed. And traffic is heavy. You're now going to have to drive a different way which will mean an extra 15-30 minutes before you arrive. You can grumble about it. That's okay. But don't stay there. This is key. Be aware of what you're feeling, even acknowledge it, and then consciously look for a new thought to gently move you in a better-feeling direction.

Find something positive in the situation. Maybe you will discover a new park or bookstore by driving this alternate route. You could see a beautiful hawk on a light pole or a deer at the edge of a field. Or you'll now have more time in the car to listen to your new playlist or audio book. Because of the change in timing, you might meet up with someone important that you wouldn't have connected with otherwise. Or now you won't cross paths with that reckless driver. You don't know. Your perspective is too close to ascertain the big picture. Try to see this as less of an inconvenience and more as a subtle adventure.

When something occurs in your life that bothers you, it's an opportunity. It's a chance to examine what you are attracting. Don't judge it. Don't beat yourself up. These opportunities are gifts that help you become more aware. And with awareness, you can redirect your focus toward nicer feeling thoughts. When you do this consistently, your dominant vibration will shift and so will your life.

The Greek philosopher Epictetus seemed to know this way back in the 2nd century when he said, *You become what you give your attention to. If you yourself don't choose what thoughts and images you expose yourself to, someone else will, and their motives may not be the highest.*

With just a little practice, you will see results. However, even after you've become adept at directing your focus, don't expect to never have another challenge in your life. You need some diversity in your daily engagements to make it interesting, and more importantly, to help you learn what it is you want (and don't want). This diversity not only adds to the spice of life, it helps us to grow and refine our ever-expanding desires.

When I was working with 35mm black and white film, the contrast between light and dark is what caused a particular image to pop. Just as these divergent aspects can help to create a stunningly gorgeous photograph, the ups and downs in your life help you to create the beautiful desires that you otherwise would not have been aware of. This is by design. With an understanding of universal magnetics, you're able to navigate troubled waters better and move through them more quickly. The universe is not reacting to what you say, it responds to your dominate vibration.

True masters control their mindset from the inside. They don't allow what is going on around them to distract from what they know is the most important thing—how they feel in their innermost being. Yet, you don't have to be a master to achieve results and to get them fast. Raising your vibration isn't difficult, it just takes practice. Selective attention is the way. Focus on things that bring you joy.

∾

I created a positive affirmation audio just for readers of this book to assist in raising and maintaining your vibrational frequency. Listen to it in the morning shortly after you awaken, throughout the day if you feel the need for a pick-me-up, or just before going to sleep.

Sign up at:

https://www.tashai.net/pages/get-free-stuff44637   for instant access.

TAKEAWAYS - CHAPTER 3

YOU CAN'T CONTINUE TO FOCUS ON SOMETHING YOU DON'T LIKE AND GET WHAT YOU WANT

1. EVERYTHING IS ENERGY AND HAS ITS OWN VIBRATION
2. THE LAW OF UNIVERSAL MAGNETICS MEANS YOU ATTRACT WHATEVER VIBRATION YOU'RE PUTTING OUT IN THE MOMENT
3. PRACTICE SELECTIVE ATTENTION: FOCUS ON WHAT YOU WANT, NOT WHAT YOU DISLIKE
4. THERE WILL ALWAYS BE UPS AND DOWNS, PERFECTION IS NOT THE GOAL. JUST MOVE IN THE DIRECTION OF YOUR CHOOSING

FOUR

THE NEWS IS NOT YOUR FRIEND

I QUIT WATCHING THE NEWS A COUPLE YEARS AGO AND MY
OUTLOOK ON LIFE HAS GOTTEN A WHOLE LOT BETTER.
 —TOM PETTY

IF IT BLEEDS, it leads. It's well known that the news outlets
tend to focus much more on negative and disturbing events
than the positive. Why? Because it sells, of course. There
have been a number of studies that point to the idea that
people react more to a negative news cycle, which in turn
translates into larger profits for the media corporations. So
the question isn't, *Why do news outlets focus predominantly
on negative subject matter?* A better question is, *Why are so
many people drawn to it?* The answer has to do with
vibrational frequency.

As we discussed in the previous chapter, our vibrational
frequency is directly affected by what we give our attention

to. The more in attunement we are with our true selves—our inner beings—the more things tend to work out for us, and the happier we feel. Unfortunately, as a society, we are taught from a young age that the best way to get what we want is to focus on those things that appear to be in opposition to our desires and then try to do something about them. We learn that we must plead our case, compete against rivals, and strive to change the thoughts and behaviors of others in order to bring them into conformity with our point of view. The law of attraction does not take sides. What we focus on expands whether our attention is on things liked or disliked.

There will always be viewpoints and events in this world that run counter to what we desire. That's life in the physical dimension, and it's truly not a bad thing. Diversity allows us to expand our understanding of what we want and don't want.

When a negative headline coaxes us to click on it, it doesn't make us wrong or bad or flawed. It's simply showing where we are in the moment. Yet, when we consistently look at things that resonate with fear and insecurity, we are temporarily obstructing who we really are and the positive changes that we desire in our lives.

In a 2014 Harvard study, it was revealed that forty percent of participants admitted that "watching, reading, or listening to the news" was one of their top life stressors. This stress results in increased levels of cortisol (a stress hormone). In small doses, cortisol is actually quite beneficial, but if you're a chronic stressor, your body produces an elevated supply of the hormone, leading to a ramped-up state of fight or flight. This can contribute to all sorts of potential mental and physical side effects including feelings of anxiety, loneliness, and hopelessness, as well as triggering post traumatic stress disorder (PTSD) symptoms.

Yet again, this all comes down to the very simple concept of what you focus on expands. Where we place our attention is a choice. Sometimes it may not feel like it, but it is. If we choose to look at things that bring us joy and pleasure, it means that at the same time we are not concentrating on subjects that brings us down. Nor are we focusing on things that cause stress.

I'm not saying we should bury our heads in the sand or ignore the struggles of others in the world. Instead, what I am saying is that we can't truly be of help to anyone else if we focus on the problem. By showing the world our alignment with our true nature of love and joy, it will have a far greater impact on society than any negative focus. True influence is imparted to others by being inspired, not through fear.

An extremely effective exercise to help you detox from a negative focus is to partake in a news fast. If you're not sure about this, dabble with it for a week and see what kind of results you get. However, if you are serious about changing your life, I suggest doing a full month of not reading or watching the news. Four weeks without the barrage of negative headlines will do you good. After that, check how you feel.

A NEWS FAST:

- No newspapers or news magazines
- No television news
- No radio news
- No online news
- No social media news

• No news talk with friends and coworkers

There are some who may question the logic of tuning out the news. They may suggest that it's irresponsible to not know what is going on in the world, that it's important to stay up-to-date on all the injustices in order to effect change. But from a law of attraction point of view, we know just the opposite is true. If you want to have a positive affect on the world, turn your attention to what you want, not what you dislike. Focusing on doing good in the world is always more powerful than stressing about what's wrong with it.

A free press is a cornerstone of a free society, and the concept of free speech is, of course, a very good one. Today, there are many reporters and news correspondents who ask the tough questions and even risk their lives to bring us the headlines that they feel we need to be aware of. Then there are also those who severely slant the content they are presenting to convey whatever message they are trying to push. In either case, the news can be seductive. It pulls on our heartstrings, riles us up, or coaxes us downward into feelings of powerlessness. The overwhelming focus is on the problems in the world, not the solutions.

If you want to change your life (and make an impact for others), a news fast is an awesome tool to get you going. No, you won't die from lack of news. Far from it. You may even get some of your life back. You certainly will find more time to do other stuff. You won't miss anything significant either. If there's something of vital importance, you will learn about it, mainly from other people telling you. But the universe will find other ways as well.

So what exactly is a news fast? Just what it sounds like.

You do not seek out news. No watching the news, no reading the news, no newspapers, no news magazines, and no online sources. No staring at the news on television while at the gym, no mainstream news in your email, no listening to news on the radio, no talking about news stories with others. Nothing. No news anywhere. What about my special case? Nope. Not for one to four weeks.

It might be enlightening to keep a little journal during your news fast. How are you feeling? Do you notice changes in your mood? Do you feel less stress? Do you have more time for other things? Are new inspirations coming to you on who you are and where you want to go in life? Stay open. Be gentle with yourself. And nudge your focus in the direction of your desires.

TAKEAWAYS - CHAPTER 4
THE NEWS IS NOT YOUR FRIEND

1. THE NEWS IS NOT REALITY. IT IS SLANTED ON THE SIDE OF THE NEGATIVE FOR SHOCK VALUE AND RATINGS
2. WATCHING THE NEWS CAN BE STRESSFUL FOR YOUR HEALTH
3. A NEWS FAST IS AN AWESOME TOOL TO DETOX YOUR MIND

FIVE

GOING FROM DESPAIR TO BLISS IS A MULTI-STEP PROCESS

A JOURNEY OF THOUSAND MILES BEGINS WITH A SINGLE STEP.

—LAO TZU

I'D LIKE to state right here that no matter who you are, no matter what your background, no matter how you are feeling, you can absolutely achieve the happiness you seek. Even if you are currently residing in the depths of despair, you can find bliss. However, going from despair to bliss does not usually occur in one giant leap, but rather in incremental steps. This doesn't mean it has to take a long time. On the contrary, the more aligned you are with your true self, the quicker you will attract the life you want. But it's about taking the steps to get you there. This was the missing piece for me. The key that made everything else possible.

Because I knew about self-development principles,

studied them, and thought I was putting them into practice, I felt I was doing everything right. Yet, the results I wanted weren't coming. I tried to *fake it until I make it,* but that wasn't getting me very far either. If I was feeling discouraged or angry, it didn't help for me to pretend that I was hopeful or optimistic. In fact, it only seemed to make me feel worse.

I was efforting in my attempts to reach my goals. The emotional gap between where I was and where I wanted to be was so large that some part of me simply could not believe it was possible. Without belief, I was sabotaging my progress. Finally I realized the answer was simple, to acknowledge where I was and start there, not from where I thought I should be. This is true for you as well.

Emotions are the Barometer

What does it mean to acknowledge where you are? How are you feeling right now? Own it. Your emotions are a great barometer for letting you know what kind of vibration you're resonating with in the present moment. Are you paying attention?

Many people are not. For some, the show of emotions was not encouraged when they were young. They have difficulty with their feelings, especially uncomfortable ones. Either through the words or behaviors of others, they learned that emotions are bad or it's weak to have feelings or other such garbage. In order to move forward, you're going to have to get in touch with your emotions again and see them for what they actually are.

Over the years, many theories have been developed in regards to emotions. Charles Darwin was an early proponent of the scientific study of emotions. He believed they were adaptations that helped both humans and animals to survive. Focusing mainly on facial expressions and what they convey, he saw these as natural evolutionary behaviors.

In the 1980s, psychologist Robert Plutchik chose eight basic emotions and grouped them into what he thought were pairs of opposites. These included joy and sadness, anger and fear, trust and disgust, and surprise and anticipation. This came to be known as a wheel of emotions. In this system, these base feelings could be mixed and combined to create other emotions, not dissimilar to how an artist might use a color wheel to produce new pigments.

More recently, psychologists Peter Salovey and John D. Mayer introduced the concept of emotional intelligence or the emotional quotient (EQ). This refers to our ability to recognize and understand our own emotions and to use this awareness to help manage life situations in positive ways.

Yet, what really are emotions? Why do we have them? What's the deal with fear? Is revenge bad? How can boredom actually be a good thing? Can we only be happy when things go our way?

I've never come across anyone who has so clearly explained the function of emotions as Abraham-Hicks has with the Emotional Guidance Scale (Esther Hicks, Jerry Hicks, *Ask and It Is Given* (Hay House, 2004), p. 114.) If you are feeling unworthy or fearful, this doesn't make you wrong, anymore than feeling hopeful or happy makes you right. Emotions are neither good nor bad. They are simply indicators of where we currently are in terms of being in alignment (or out of alignment) with our true selves.

Think of the Emotional Guidance Scale as a ladder with

each rung representing a distinct vibratory frequency. At the top are those emotions that are in greatest alignment with who you really are—such as love, joy, and freedom. Life just seems to hum along when you reside in this upper third. In the middle, things feel less clear, less engaging. And yet, if you find yourself in this emotional region, take heart! The middle third of the scale is a great place to be because it's not much of a reach to those better feeling emotions. You're not far! At the bottom of the scale are ones where we feel most disconnected—fear, depression, and powerlessness. We've all felt these at one point or another. That's what it means to be human. In the heat of the moment when you find yourself in the depths of despair, making a climb up to hopefulness or enthusiasm can feel like an impossible task. But I promise you it is not. How do you climb a ladder? One rung at a time. The further we go, the greater the empowerment we feel. With each and every rung, you will be taking back your power and realigning more and more with who you really are.

The following is adapted from the Abraham-Hicks Emotional Guidance Scale:

Upper Third of the Ladder

*

1. Joy/Unconditional Love
2. Enthusiasm
3. Belief
4. Optimism
5. Hopefulness

6. Satisfaction

Middle Third of the Ladder

*

7. Boredom
8. Pessimism
9. Frustration/Impatience
10. Overrun
11. Disappointment
12. Doubt
13. Worry

Lower Third of the Ladder

*

14. Blame
15. Anger
16. Revenge
17. Hatred
18. Jealousy
19. Guilt/Unworthiness
20. Fear/Despair/Powerlessness

Note: Of course, there are more emotions than just these. Feel free to add any others at the appropriate place if needed.

So how does this work? At any point in your day, you can take a moment to check in on your emotional state. With just a little practice, you will find yourself getting quite good at identifying where you are on the ladder. If it's a low vibrational place and you want to improve your outlook, then identifying where you are is the first step. Next, give yourself permission: *It's okay for me to feel better.*

For example, if you're experiencing pangs of unworthiness, then according to the scale, the next step up is actually jealousy, a higher vibration. Feeling unworthy, you may say something to yourself like, *I'll never have the house of my dreams because I don't deserve it.* But moving up a rung to jealousy is more empowering. *I'm so jealous of those rich people in their fancy homes.* I don't recommend staying at this level, but it is a step in the right direction. The goal is to align with a better feeling vibration because like attracts like.

It is important to remember that making a move from jealously to, say, a state of joy in one step is usually too far of a leap for most people. So, give yourself a break as you climb upwards. Take it step by step and allow yourself to feel every emotion as you go. If you try to force a sense of joy while still on a lower rung, it will feel inauthentic and false, and you will likely not be able to truly advance. Climbing the ladder requires belief. If it doesn't feel real to you, then how can it become a reality?

Let me reiterate, emotions are neither good or bad. They are simply your own built-in gauge that lets you know where you're hanging out vibrationally at any point in time. And when I speak of higher and lower vibrations, I'm not referring to the electrical activity of the human brain. When researchers observe brain wave frequencies, they are measuring tiny electrical charges from the brain cells. The more relaxed a person is, the lower or slower the brain wave frequency. A person in deep meditation or sleep may show slow moving waves associated with the delta state.

This is a measurement of what is going on inside the physical brain.

However, the frequency of emotions is different. An emotion is not a physical function. It most certainly can and does affect our physical state in a very real way, but the vibration of an emotion is part of the non-physical world. So when I refer to a higher frequency, I'm referring to an emotion that is more in alignment with our natural state of being such as feelings of joy and empowerment. A lower frequency emotion would obviously land somewhere further down the ladder.

With that said, what if you are not in touch with your emotions? You look at the Emotional Guidance Scale and you really don't know what you are feeling. How do you reconnect? In the beginning, I don't feel it's necessary to pinpoint the exact emotional state that you may be experiencing. Just feel around until you become aware of the general vicinity of where you land. Are you closer to lowest frequency of despair and powerlessness? Or the highest, happiness and freedom? With only a little practice, your recognition of what you are feeling will become more keen.

If you need help identifying your current emotional state, here are a couple of exercises to try.

Name That Emotion

You probably don't have much trouble identifying the more overt ones like fear, sadness, anger, or bliss. So when you notice that you're having an intense reaction to something, stop and name that feeling. Just bringing your attention to it is a powerful step toward raising your vibration. Check in with yourself at various times during the day and practice identifying what you are feeling. While intense emotions may catch our attention, there are also those nuanced emotions that are less often recognized. Unworthiness, worry, doubt, disappointment. We may have a sensation of something nagging at us, an uncomfortable feeling, and yet, we're not noticing or paying attention to what is going on inside. So it just sort of lingers and festers. It's much better to stop and identify what it is.

Listen to Your Body

Another avenue for discovering your emotional state is through the sensations in your body. Take a deep breath. How is your body feeling right now? Often we will experience a physical sensation associated with an emotion. For example, fear is commonly felt in the vicinity of the stomach, diaphragm, or chest. These sensations can include tightness, numbness, fluttering, or nausea. Happiness can be felt as a warming sensation either in the heart area or spreading throughout the whole body. Obviously different people will have their own unique physical sensations. You can learn the language of yours. If you slow down and listen, your body will tell you what you are feeling.

So why is this important? I know you get that emotions are vibrations, and that higher frequencies feel better. Yet, what we are looking for is the baseline of your life. Where do you regularly hang out? Sadness? Anger? Worry? Boredom? Or are you optimistic most of the time? What's your norm?

There will always be ups and downs in life, but if your modus operandi leans towards the lower half of the scale, you will attract more of this into your life. If you want to break free of this same old same old, then make a conscious effort to move up the ladder step by step.

Snap a picture of the emotional scale from earlier in this chapter and keep it with you on your phone. Then the next time you find yourself out of sorts, take a few minutes to hone in on what you are feeling. Try to pinpoint the emotion on the scale.

Example One

Step 1. Acknowledge where you are by saying what you truly feel. *I am feeling angry because I am 40 years old, I'm smart, and yet I haven't got my money situation where I want it. I'm angry at my boss for not respecting me: I'm angry at myself for being in this situation. I'm just so angry.*

Step 2. Reach for the next higher emotion which in this case is blame. *I blame my parents for not preparing me better. They weren't good with money so I feel like I can't be.*

Step 3. Next rung. Worry. *I'm worried that I'm a failure, and I won't have enough money when I retire.*

Step 4. Doubt. *I doubt that things are ever going to change for me. I'm still in the same circumstances as I always have been. I haven't made any progress at all.*

Step 5. Disappointment. *I'm disappointed in myself for allowing me to get in this situation.*

. . .

This is climbing the ladder step by step. Notice that you don't have to spend a lot of time on each emotion. Just state how you feel and move up to a higher and higher frequency.

The goal is to feel better. The better you feel, the more you will attract things into your life that match this vibration. And the more you do this, the easier it gets. However, you must be honest with yourself. If you reach for a higher emotion, but you honestly can't feel it, then don't pretend. You have to believe what you say for this to work.

In the example above, our subject started out angry and climbed the ladder to disappointment. Disappointment may not seem like a good place to stop, but it truly is a better feeling vibration than anger. She could have continued all the way up to happiness if it felt right.

This next example actually happened to my husband just recently. Robert has been helping me with the edit of this book, and in particular, the latest draft of this chapter on emotions. The universe always finds ways of sneaking in life examples just at the appropriate time.

He's been working a lot of overtime at his job lately, and the other night when he came home, it was late and he was tired. He had planned to do up some dishes that had piled up for a day and a half, plus pick up some clutter he'd left around the house. But now all he wanted to do was to eat and go to sleep. I could tell he was in a mood.

After dinner, he was getting ready for bed, and we sat and talked a bit. The conversation came around to the topic of being happy and how all that matters is being happy, no matter what. Something seemed to free up in him to the point where he was willing to run through the emotional scale. It didn't take long to identify the emotion he was feeling—overrun.

Example Two

Step 1. Overrun. *I feel overworked and exhausted, I and have no energy to do anything. All I want is to go to bed.*

Step 2. Frustration. *I feel so frustrated that my life is still the way it is. Working long hours, it doesn't feel like things are getting any better.*

Step 3. Pessimism. *Things won't change in my life, not enough to make a difference. I don't see how things will ever change.*

Step 4. Boredom. *I give up. All I want to do is veg out, watch TV, and eat carbs.*

Step 5. Satisfaction. *You know, I can actually see there have been some changes in my life. I can be satisfied with the good things I can see in my life right now. Life is good.*

At this point, my husband—who just a few minutes before was no more than a walking zombie heading to bed—suddenly popped up, without any prodding from me, and began picking up the clutter off the floor. He then proceeded to the kitchen and started on the dishes, with the caveat that he'd just a do a few before bed. He called me in so he could continue on the emotion scale.

This was a guy who, after a 14-hour day at work, had no energy left in his body. Yet, within a few minutes of climbing a few emotional rungs, he was suddenly energized. His exhaustion had evaporated. The tone in his voice was transformed. While he washed the dishes, he continued up the ladder.

Step 6. Hopefulness. *I feel hopeful that things are going to get better, that my life situation will improve, and I'll be able to do more of the things that I want.*

The next rung on the ladder is optimism. It's interesting to note that when he tried it on for size, he couldn't make it fit. He attempted a statement about being optimistic but wavered because it didn't feel real. Some part of him simply wasn't ready to believe it. Going beyond this point on the emotional scale would not have been helpful. So he left it at hopefulness, which is absolutely fine. He got to the upper part of the scale, he felt better, and that's all that matters.

And by the way, he ended up doing all of the dishes, then stayed up for another hour working with me on the edit of this chapter. Boom! This shit works!

You don't have to make a giant leap from despair to happiness to effect real change in your life. Just becoming aware of where you are emotionally will bring you relief. Then climbing a few rungs on the ladder will make you feel even lighter.

Practice climbing this emotional ladder often. Get the hang of it. If you do, you will notice more often than not that your starting place on the scale will be higher than it was before when dealing with the same subject matter. That's real progress baby! This consistency in living at higher emotional levels will help bring about the changes you are looking for in life. And just as important, you will feel better along your journey, no matter where you are.

TAKEAWAYS - CHAPTER 5

GOING FROM DESPAIR TO BLISS IS A MULTI-STEP PROCESS

1. START WHERE YOU ARE, DON'T FAKE IT UNTIL YOU MAKE IT
2. IDENTIFY THE EMOTION YOU ARE FEELING IN THIS MOMENT
3. FIND WHERE YOU MOST OFTEN "HANG OUT" ON THE EMOTIONAL SCALE
4. CONSCIOUSLY, STEP-BY-STEP, MOVE UP THE RUNGS AS FAR AS YOU CAN GO UNTIL YOU'VE REACHED A STOPPING POINT

SIX

WHAT'S WRONG WITH YOU OR WHY CAN'T YOU MAINTAIN YOUR NEW VIBRATION?

If you want to find the secrets of the universe, think in terms of energy, frequency, and vibration.
—Nikola Tesla

As your awareness expands and you turn your focus towards things wanted, your vibration will rise. With a higher emotional baseline, things will feel like they are finally coming together for you. The more you resonate with higher frequency emotions, the more your physical surroundings will begin to reflect this back to you. But life is life. And just because you feel fantastic today, tomorrow could bring new challenges. Your boss could catch you off guard with criticism of your new project. You throw yourself out of kilter and tumble down the emotional rabbit hole into a bout of anger and discouragement.

You Are Worthy

Why can't you maintain your high vibe feelings? What's wrong with you? First off, there is nothing wrong with you. You are worthy of your dreams and aspirations no matter where you are now. Secondly, no one here on the earth plane maintains feelings of joy and bliss one hundred percent of the time. Becoming a smiley-face automaton is not the goal.

It's natural to experience emotional highs and lows. It's even by design, on purpose. Life in the physical world is meant for expansion, continual growth, and the redefining of desires. This means you will encounter things you don't like, yes, but it also means these very same things will help you to become clearer on what you do want and desire. You will continually refine these wants and desires as long as you are here.

Even masters have their days. They may not experience the same kind of emotional rollercoaster ride that you and I might, especially on our *bad* days. Yet, they still move up and down the range of emotions as all humans do. However, a master understands that emotions are nothing more than guideposts, letting us know where you are in the moment. Try to remember this if you experience an unpleasant reaction to something in your life. Don't beat yourself up. You didn't fail at anything.

Look at it like this, you see a sign on the side of the road saying *Elmhurst Lane*. Are you upset at yourself when you see the sign? Or is it just a guidepost to let you know where you are? It's the same with emotions. So if you don't want to be on Elmhurst Lane, at least you know where you are, and now you're free to do something about it.

Issues only arise when we start judging ourselves for

where we are. *I'm on Elmhurst again! How could I be back here*? Or *Elmhurst Lane is soooo long! I thought I'd be to my destination by now.* You get my meaning. Being where you are and feeling what you are feeling is not a problem until you think it defines something about your worth as a person.

You are worthy no matter what you think you have or haven't accomplished in your life so far. You are where you have intended to be. If you want something different, intend differently. Just acknowledge where you are and start from there. It's counterproductive to pretend you are in a place you aren't. Use the emotional ladder from the previous chapter to move towards the frequencies that will bring you what you want.

It's Okay to Feel a Bit Itchy

If you are accustomed to hanging out at a certain vibrational level, there could be an adjustment period as you do the work and begin to inhabit new, higher emotional frequencies. Most often you will feel amazing, freer and lighter than ever at these new levels. But because of old habitual patterns, it's also possible that you could feel a little strange or uncomfortable on occasion, like you may not know quite what to do with yourself. With more than the usual amount of energy in your body, you might feel somewhat anxious or jittery, a bit *itchy*.

It's okay. You will adjust as you get more comfortable in your new skin. You will acclimate and life around you will start to adapt to your new vibe also. Give yourself permission to feel a bit unsettled for a while. You're now walking in new shoes, allow some time to break them in.

Dr. Wayne Dyer once used the analogy of an old pair of

nylon running shorts to illustrate a valuable insight into the expanding of our minds to new horizons. Once the fabric is stretched beyond a certain point, it can never go back to what it once was. The same is true for us. When we expand our lives beyond what we've known, we can never fully go back to what we were. Sure, some part of us may cling to the old comfort zone, but the real excitement is found by looking forward.

Once integrated, your new vibe will become your new standard and will be as comfortable and natural as your favorite pair of shoes.

Before we go on the the next chapter, I want you to keep in mind there is no race to the finish line. There is no finish line. Even death is not the end of you. You are an eternal being. There's always more to experience. More to release, more to learn, more discoveries to be had, more laughter, more desires, more money, more bliss. More. And you get to choose the direction of your more.

TAKEAWAYS - CHAPTER 6

WHAT'S WRONG WITH YOU OR WHY CAN'T YOU MAINTAIN YOUR VIBRATION?

1. There is nothing wrong with you
2. Being happy 100% of the time is not the goal
3. Emotions are just guideposts to let you know where you are in any given moment
4. Transitioning to higher levels may at first feel a bit strange or *itchy*

SEVEN

THE LIVING WORLD

I ONLY WENT OUT FOR A WALK, AND FINALLY CONCLUDED
TO STAY OUT TILL SUNDOWN, FOR GOING OUT, I FOUND,
WAS REALLY GOING IN.

—JOHN MUIR

I LIVE IN A CITY, yet because of the forethought of those who came before, I have access to a multitude of parks, bike paths, hiking trails, public forests, and nature preserves. I love visiting wild natural areas and vacationing at national parks, which are some of my favorite places on the planet.

Robert and I have explored the Florida Everglades and camped on the beach in the Keys, soaking up the scents and sounds of the Atlantic Ocean. We've hiked under the canopy of the Redwoods of Northern California and scrambled amongst the tide pools of Point Reyes National Seashore. We've absorbed the backcountry silence and solitude of the Utah Canyonlands as we searched for prehistoric pictographs. We awoke one morning in the Black Hills of South Dakota to discover a spring snow storm had completely blanketed the landscape, including the huge bull bison who had wandered into our space during the night. There he was sleeping near us, looking like a big boulder covered in snow.

Just for readers of *Fill the Gap*, see exclusive photos from this and other stories in this book. Go to my website to get the link:

https://www.tashai.net/pages/get-free-stuff44637

Setting foot in nature is by far one of the purest and easiest ways of raising (or maintaining) your high vibration and syncing with your inner being. The natural world is attuned to the highest vibratory frequencies. All we have to do to connect is let go. Allow it in. Naturalist and nature essayist, John Burroughs wrote, *I go to nature to be soothed and healed, and to have my senses put in order.*

There Are No Chance Encounters

Nature's healing effect can be found everywhere, from the grandiose to the microscopic, even in the most desolate of urban areas. Twice a week, my husband's job requires him to visit a business which has a huge wasteland of a parking lot leading up to the entrance of the building. And nearly every time he arrives, a small group of crows flies in to welcome him. They circle above before coming in for a landing. The sound of caws and wing flaps fill the asphalt environs. The birds seem genuinely pleased to see his arrival. And the feeling is mutual. An onlooker might suggest that the flock is simply associating humans with the possibility of a discarded food scrap to scavenge.

(Robert does not feed the crows.) The onlooker would be missing the true nature of this interaction.

From a place of deep inner knowing, Robert understands that the crows aren't just there by happenstance. They've come to rendezvous with him, to share in a moment of fun and connection, to remind him—in amongst all the noise and chaos of the modern world—of who he really is. On an intuitive level, he talks to them and they back. Then they go on their way. The natural world is always there, pointing us towards our own transcendent essence. We are more than just physical bodies, and nature will call us to that aspect of ourselves every time, if we let it.

Look around when you're heading to work or running errands. Notice animal behavior. Birds on a wire, squirrels hanging from branches, insects buzzing in the trees. Observe the grasses gently blowing in the wind, the weeds poking up through the sidewalk. At first glance, these everyday encounters may seem routine and uninspiring. But they're there for you.

If you allow it, both flora and fauna will co-create with you, show off for you, let you witness their behavior, even communicate non-verbally with you. There are no chance sightings. The songbird that flew by or the flower in bloom, they came to play with you. The Universe is alive and is always looking to draw you back, back to an awareness of the purity of who you really are. When something in nature catches your attention, you're connecting with it because your vibration calls it to you. Not by chance. The higher your vibration, the deeper the connection; the higher your frequency, the more you will see. In fact, you will observe things that simply weren't available to you when you were resonating further down on the emotional ladder.

Going Deeper

Escaping from the noise, traffic, and hustle and bustle may not always be as uncomplicated as we'd like, but it's worth it. I love to be around people. Although I also need the balance of quality solitariness. There is great reward in getting away from the crowds from time to time. I'm talking wild nature, not just a campground full of hundreds of others, with yelling and laughing, blaring music and plenty of commotion. Don't get me wrong, this type of outdoor activity can be loads of fun. I've partaken in the socializing campground atmosphere on many occasions.

However, getting out into the deeper solitude has a cleansing effect beyond what words can accurately describe. In a scene from the movie, *Joe Verses the Volcano*, Joe (played by Tom Hanks) and Patricia (Meg Ryan) are out under the stars in the middle of a calm Pacific Ocean. They're on a sailboat owned by Patricia's father. She tells Joe that her father has agreed to give her the boat; all she has to do in return is deliver Joe to the remote island of Waponi Woo, the one with the big volcano. Joe, not quite comprehending why Patricia would want or need a boat, asks her where she would go once it's hers. She replies, *Away from the things of man.*

City Jitters

When Robert and I prepare for a trip, there's often a frenzy of activity as the departure date draws near—shopping, packing, pet sitters, last-minute work-related wrap-ups, etc. So by the time we finally arrive at our destination, we have what I call the *city jitters*. We start to notice it after our camp is set up, when all the activity settles down. There's this weird sensation of not knowing what to do next. No phones, no schedules, no deadlines. It's almost a feeling of boredom. *I've come all the way here, I'm out in the middle of nowhere, and there's nothing to do!* It usually takes a day for us to unwind.

Considering how wired the life was that we just left behind, experiencing city jitters is not overly surprising. What might be surprising, though, is the idea that boredom is not a bad thing. As we know from chapter 5 of this book, boredom is only one step below contentment on the Emotional Guidance Scale. It's fun and inspiring to observe just how precise the law of attraction is—like a mathematical equation. As we settle into our new outdoor surroundings, like clockwork, our vibrational frequencies begin to rise. Any lingering evidence of boredom then must dissipate into contentment, and if we allow it, on up the ladder until we find ourselves in bliss. It's a universal principle. You don't have to work at it. Simply relax and let it happen naturally.

Reconnecting

I've done pilgrimages into nature for most of my life, and I always return refreshed after such sabbaticals. The vivid and pleasant memories from these excursions continue to fill me with joy, as if they happened only yesterday.

On one such trip, I spent several nights at Devils Tower National Monument in Wyoming. You probably recall it from Steven Spielberg's sci-fi classic film, *Close Encounters of the Third Kind*. The central feature of the park is what geologists refer to as a magma intrusion. Millions of years ago, lava welled up underground and hardened before making it to the surface. Slowly over time, the sedimentary rock above weathered away, leaving exposed the harder igneous rock that is the tower today.

It's quite striking to look upon, rising up out of the Great Plains landscape. For those who are sensitive to it, this natural rock monolith emanates a strong energetic aura, at once peaceful and powerful. It's a sacred place for numerous Native American tribes and other people as well.

Before this trip to the tower, I had been experiencing a lot of work-related stress and was in real need of decompressing. During the summer months, daytime visitation to the monument is bustling; the main road up to the visitor center often has a steady stream of traffic. Situated near the base of the boulder field that surrounds the tower is the visitor center. It's the jumping off spot for hiking the loop trail that encircles this gigantic geologic feature. It's a very pleasant trail but, again, the foot traffic is heavy on peak days.

So I chose to head further out, away from the main road and the curious tourists, to a more remote trail. I came upon the perfect quiet spot with a spectacular view of the tower, and I had the place to myself. It was a hot Wyoming day, the sun was a bit brutal, which made the gentle breeze and the shade of a ponderosa pine feel like heaven. I laid a blanket on the ground, settled in, and stayed for hours. Sometimes sitting, sometimes laying, always soaking in the rhythm of the nature around me.

I removed my hiking boots and socks, and rested my bare feet on the ground, not only because it felt delectable to do so, but also so I could take advantage of the Earth's electrical charge (more on this in a bit). It was an amazing afternoon. I could feel my stress melting away little by little as my vibration rose. As I relaxed deeper and deeper, my connection with the world around me became more tangible.

I listened to the sound of the wind in the pines, observed a bumble bee on its rounds, and tracked the shifting patterns of clouds as they encountered the tower. I even watched with interest as a man and woman down in the valley carried a chaise lounge out into the field, pulled out a camera and tripod, and snapped a few photos of themselves with the tower as a backdrop—an Instagram moment for sure. Then just as quickly as they had appeared, they picked up the couch and returned to whence they came. Truly a strange sight. It was a beautiful day.

When I finally headed back down, I was alive and renewed. At my campsite that night, my spirit felt cleansed. My emotional vibrational frequency had come into sync with the natural world, and I was in a state of bliss.

One of my favorite things to do is to get into some wild area where I may only see one or two other people on a trail or off in the distance, or maybe not another person all day. On another trip, Robert and I traveled to Tennessee to experience Smoky Mountains National Park. Although the park on average receives well over ten million visitors per year, you can set up reservations in advance to stay in the backcountry. Once you hit the trail, the number of people you encounter dramatically decreases.

After backpacking a few hours in the rain, and passing numerous individuals and small groups of hikers, the number of people we encountered steadily dwindled until we were no longer seeing anyone else. We finally arrived at our backcountry camp where we planned to stay for a couple of nights. There were three or four other designated sites at this location, but we had the entire place to ourselves, which surprised and delighted us.

The morning of the next day was beautiful, clear and sunny. We decided to explore off-trail, just wandering and letting our hearts lead wherever they may. Coming upon a stream flowing down through a rocky ravine, we knew we had to follow it. It was springtime, the temperatures were comfortably pleasant, no biting bugs, and all the plants and trees still sported that beautiful spring green glow! The sights, sounds, and smells of the forest were intoxicating.

I don't remember what inspired us to remove our clothes. It might have been the tranquilizing melody of the bubbling water combined with the song of migrating warblers. Whatever it was, we slipped out of our garments as effortlessly as one might drop a bathrobe before stepping into an inviting bubble bath. We hadn't seen or heard any humans all morning. Tucking our clothes and shoes at the base of a big maple tree, we continued our exploratory hike down the stream—butt naked.

Now I don't want to give the wrong impression here. Robert and I are not nudists. I don't have anything against people who are, but this wasn't normal public behavior for us. We were just so moved by the sheer delight and beauty of our surroundings that the removal of our clothes simply felt like the thing to do in that moment. Well that moment turned into an all-day event!

It really didn't take long before walking around naked felt utterly natural and comfortable. We spent hours exploring the stream, basking on rock slabs, and observing fish, birds and insects in and about the water. It was another day of bliss.

Immersing yourself in nature not only purges the mind, it also has beneficial effects on the body—in addition to the obvious one of physical exercise. When we walk or sit on the ground in a natural setting with bare feet (or bare bottoms), our bodies profit from the direct physical contact with the Earth's natural electrical charge. This idea even has a name, Earthing, and research shows that test subjects do experience improved physiological balance, pain reduction, deeper sleep, and more—simply by going barefoot. From a vibrational point of view, this is not surprising. If sticking your toes in the sand makes you feel happy, the cells of your body will follow suit.

In addition, any natural area that emits a high negative ion count can also benefit us. Negative ions are molecules that have been charged with electricity. They are measurable, and in nature, they are found in abundance at some of the most scenic locales on the planet. In the mountains, at the beach, around waterfalls and fast moving streams, and in the air after thunderstorms. While scientific research still needs to be done on the deeper effects of negative ions, there have been studies showing positive health benefits such as the relief from depression. As a person who has personally visited numerous areas of high negative ionization, the feeling is nothing short of euphoric. We certainly felt it at our stream oasis in the Smoky Mountains.

Hours had passed and the sun was getting lower through the trees. We were still naked. The experience was so freeing. I was surprised at just how natural and normal it felt, even though I'd never been nude outside before. After a full day without my clothes, it truly was strange putting them back on. This experience did not turn me into a nudist, but I loved the feeling it gave me. Being in the buff and comfortable in nature opened my eyes. It made me appreciate my body as a beautiful avatar for my soul, and appreciate how it allows me to experience this world of the physical.

We had the whole clothing-optional day to ourselves. It wasn't until we hiked back to our camp that we came across another group of backpackers; they were just arriving. Divine timing. When you are happy and free, you're vibrating at the upper part of the emotional ladder. And things simply work out for you more often. Even in times of apparent difficulty and struggle, if you look for it, you will find reassurance and guidance emanating from the nature around you. Something I experienced on yet another excursion.

Nature Has Your Back If You Allow It

Rocky Mountain National Park was like home to us, having lived in Colorado for several years. We visited the park many times, although we'd never hiked this particular section before. Robert and I had several layers of clothing on our bodies and ample food and water in our packs because the trail would take us most of the day to complete. No cellphones though (they weren't widely available yet).

We were dropped off at the furtherest trailhead at around 9,500 feet above sea level. The route would be rocky and mostly downhill, descending over 1000 feet to the far trailhead where our vehicle was parked. We left early in the morning to insure we made it back before any late afternoon thunderstorm blew in, a common occurrence in the summer months.

The air was fresh and cold at this elevation. The scenery was beautiful, and we were both in high spirits. Physically, we were in decent shape, having walked regularly in the mountains. Although, this route was more rugged and started higher in elevation than what we were used to.

Things were going swimmingly until about halfway

through the hike when I noticed my knees starting to stiffen up from the mostly-downhill grade of the trail. Then we came to a glacial stream crossing. The water wasn't too deep, about calf-high, but as the word *glacial* implies, it was ice cold. In hindsight, we probably should have left our boots on and just motored through it. We were wearing wool hiking socks, our feet would have been wet, but warm still.

Taking off our shoes and socks and rolling up our pant legs, we waded in. The shock of that frigid water on my bare feet and calves chilled me to the bone. I felt the muscles in my legs tightening to the point of real pain. Thankfully, it wasn't too wide of a stream so I was out and on the other side as quick as possible. The pain subsided, but the muscle stiffness did not.

Drying off in a hurry, I was warmed up soon enough with socks and boots back on. We stopped for lunch, and I tried some yoga poses to stretch my legs. This didn't help, though. The tightness lingered.

The descent down the trail proved slower and more difficult than expected. Sections of the trail cut through rocky outcrops where the next footfall may be several feet below. This steep downward movement only amplified the rigid feeling in my knees. It felt as if the joints had rusted stiff. They were really starting to hurt and were refusing to bend anymore. We had miles to go, and the terrain would have made it extremely difficult for Robert to carry me and our full packs.

There was still plenty of daylight left, but we had to press on because late afternoon storm clouds were now brewing. We could see them coming and knew we had to get off the mountain soon. The chance of a lightning strike is a very real thing, and being exposed in the mountains during a thunderstorm is not the best place to find yourself.

Because I was having such a difficult time, I wan't sure that I would make it into the valley before the storm hit. Robert was carrying both of our packs, and I told him to go on some and not wait for me. He did go off to scout the trail ahead but then would wait until I caught up again before going further.

At this point, I had no idea how far it was to the trail's end and our vehicle. I was feeling annoyed at my legs for not being up for this hike. And then a few rain drops began to splash down on me. I was seriously wavering on the edge of an emotional downturn when I suddenly heard a buzzing noise.

I know that sound! It was the distinct buzz created by the wings of a hummingbird. Then I saw him, a male broad-tailed hummer with his brightly colored rose-magenta throat patch. It zoomed right up to me, stared for a moment, flitted back and forth, then off he went. A hummingbird! First one I'd seen since moving to Colorado. He showed up for me at the moment I needed him most, and his message was simple but clear, *It will be all right. Just enjoy the trail as you can.* He had come along *for me*, and I knew it with all my heart. It was a non-verbal vibrational communication where the hummer and my inner being connected. My spirit immediately lifted!

The trail began to level out more, and for the moment, the rain had stopped. The stream was now running along side, and I could see farther up ahead. There was Robert waiting for me. I was feeling lighter again when suddenly a wave of sound rose up from behind and surrounded me, seemingly coming from everywhere at once.

At least 15 more hummers swarmed around my head,

darting from me to the stream and back again. They stayed for a moment, then off they went down the trail. What an experience! I love hummingbirds and to see and hear so many surrounding me in their wild habitat was pure euphoria. A weight had been lifted and my legs actually felt somewhat better. Around another bend, Robert and I met other hikers, the first we'd encountered all day. They too had seen the hummers, and we all talked about it with great elation. Another few minutes of walking and up ahead we could see the parking area and our vehicle. We had made it back before the storm, but even more important, the hummers helped me to realign with my inner being when I needed it most.

A pilgrimage into the backcountry is like good medicine. However you don't need to go to the wilderness to feel the benefits of the natural world. It's all around us, even if you live in an apartment in the city. Look for it and nature will find you. The rejuvenating benefits cannot be overstated.

Let it in.

TAKEAWAYS - CHAPTER 7
THE LIVING WORLD

1. THE FLORA AND FAUNA, THE WIND AND ROCKS ARE ALL CALLING YOU BACK TO WHO YOU REALLY ARE
2. SPENDING TIME OUT INTO NATURE NATURALLY RAISES YOUR VIBRATION ON THE EMOTIONAL LADDER
3. THE EARTH'S ELECTRICAL CHARGE AND NEGATIVE IONS CAN HAVE POSITIVE EFFECTS ON BOTH YOUR BODY AND MIND, RELIEVING STRESS AND CLEANSING YOUR SPIRIT
4. YOU CAN EXPERIENCE THE CALMING EFFECTS OF NATURE EVEN IN THE MOST URBAN OF SETTINGS

EIGHT

DECLUTTERING

HAVE NOTHING IN YOUR HOME THAT YOU DO NOT KNOW TO
BE USEFUL OR BELIEVE TO BE BEAUTIFUL.
　　—WILLIAM MORRIS

I'VE HAD a lot of encounters with clutter in my life...I mean a lot! My father was a massive hoarder, truly one of the best. So was my father-in-law. Then there was an old boss of mine; she could have given them both a run for their money. We had a close friend who, too, floundered under the weight of his accumulations. There were others as well.

As I sat down to write this chapter, it dawned on me the sheer number of people I've personally known who've suffered from an extreme hoarding disorder. Is this normal? I don't know. Are you also able to name half a dozen or more hardcore hoarders in your life?

While these folks make easy the argument for

decluttering, I'm not just focusing on hoarding here. In fact, a hoarder is simply someone who has allowed their clutter to build up over time to the point of dysfunction. Most all of us are not hoarders, yet we still could benefit from some form of cleanup.

I believe the subject of reducing clutter in our personal lives is so important that I'm writing an entire book on it to help people achieve their decluttering goals. Learn more at: https://tashai.net

What exactly is clutter? Merriam-Webster's dictionary defines clutter as *a crowded or confused mass or collection of scattered or disordered things that impede movement or reduce effectiveness.* In addition, I would say that clutter is a result of dwelling too often in a low frequency emotional state.

The most obvious form of clutter is, of course, the physical stuff that accumulates in our lives. But there are other forms too—digital, energetic, mental. Addressing any one of these areas will indeed have a positive effect on all the others. The boost you get from decluttering will be palpable. Whenever you find yourself feeling stuck or in a rut, pick an area of your life—whatever feels easiest—and dive in. Here's a few examples below.

Digital Clutter

Let's start with your digital life. Is the desktop on your computer a mess? Is your operating system bogging down? Outdated files clogging up your hard drive? How many photos are on your smartphone that you'll never look at again? Set aside some time. Organize your desktop. Update your operating system. Delete old files you no longer need, and back up the rest onto an external drive or the cloud. Clean up your phone. Go through the old photos, videos and songs you no longer want. Remove unused apps. It's such a simple task, but you will feel lighter, freer.

Energetic Clutter

All forms of decluttering are energetic at some level. The world after all is made up of vibrating molecular particles. But there are times when things feel stale or in need of a cleansing. A new home, an old car, jewelry inherited from your grandmother, new crystals you purchased at the rock shop, a pair of jeans from the thrift store. Whenever something feels a little vibrationally off or unclean, do a smudging ritual. Light a sage bundle or a piece of palo santo tree wood. Each produces a pleasant smelling scent.

As you bathe your object or chosen space with the smoke, it's important to have the intention in mind that you are cleansing it, just as if it were being washed in water, removing the *energetic soot*.

Alternatively, if it won't ruin the item in question, you can leave it outside to soak up the sunlight for a few days or to bathe in the moonlight overnight. Again, set your intention for it to be cleansed.

You are giving it a fresh start. This act of bathing your object or space in smoke or natural light directs your focus and raises *your* vibration. And that's the point of all this.

Mental Clutter

My definition of mental clutter is a thought that makes you feel worse. Period. Doesn't matter what it is, who it's about, if it's true or not. If it pushed you down a rung on the emotional ladder, then it's clutter. As previously mentioned, your emotions are guideposts. They indicate *where* you are vibrationally. Your thoughts, on the other hand, are *how* you got there. Are you flying high or feeling low?

Cleaning up your mental clutter is not about clearing out negative thoughts. Have you tried it? Doesn't work. If you focus on not thinking about something, that something just ends up becoming the focal point of your thoughts. Instead, gently allow yourself to turn your attention to another subject altogether. Don't fight against what you don't want. Go towards what you do want, towards a thought that makes you feel good, Anything. Puppies, babies, motorcycles, whatever works for you.

Physical Clutter

You may not be a hoarder, but if you're like most of us, you still have physical clutter somewhere in your life. It could be something as simple as unopened mail sitting on the kitchen counter for the past week or a two-days worth of dirty dishes in the sink. If there's a larger issue, you might own too much stuff for the size of your home. The more serious clutter scenarios could include stacks of outdated, unread magazines or newspapers in the living room; broken appliances and unwanted furniture in the garage; or clothes two sizes too small in the spare bedroom closet.

If you think you don't have any clutter, try looking with fresh eyes. A good way to do this is to snap a photo of your space. Often this new perspective will give you clues into your clutter situation, allowing you to see problem areas that you couldn't recognize while physically standing in the room. Clean out everything unwanted, unneeded, unused, broken, and outgrown.

For example, you can start by picking up and putting

away anything that is out of place. Maybe the clean laundry has been sitting in the basket for three days and you're grabbing clothes to wear from the pile rather than opening your dresser. Or you didn't bother to put your coat and shoes in the closet when you came home last night. Put them away.

Are you holding onto things you no longer use? Books, magazines, jewelry, clothes, dishes, appliances, furniture. If you've lived in the same home for more than five years, I guarantee you have some purging to do. Check everywhere —your basement, attic, garden shed, storage unit, and your vehicles. Take that stuff to a recycle center, a thrift shop, or sell it online. Let someone else enjoy and benefit from the things you no longer use. Do this often. Decluttering is not a *one and done* practice. It's a lifelong exercise, and it is something you will come to look forward to because of the unmistakeable energy boost it bestows.

Deep Clean

Then there is the deep clean, something you do every few years. With a deep clean, you go through absolutely everything you own. Everything is examined with this question in mind, *Is this furthering my life or holding me back?* Think as William Morris, *Is this thing beautiful or useful in my life?* If not, it goes.

A good way to start a deep clean is to pretend you are moving to a new house, but there will be no hiring of professional packers in this scenario. Imagine that you have to pack up your belongings on your own. Would you really want to take all those things with you? What would you keep? And what can you live without?

Anytime you are feeling stuck or uninspired, look around for clutter you can purge. Doesn't matter if it's digital, energetic, mental or actual physical clutter—clear it. You not only gain the obvious benefit of less clutter in your space, but you also open yourself to new and exciting things on the horizon. Clearing at any stage can have astonishing restorative effects. It's truly a breath of fresh air.

Some of us think holding on makes us strong, but sometimes it is letting go.
—Herman Hesse

TAKEAWAYS - CHAPTER 8

DECLUTTERING

1. HOARDERS ARE JUST PEOPLE WHO HAVE ALLOWED THEIR CLUTTER TO ESCALATE TO THE POINT OF DISFUNCTION
2. THERE ARE DIFFERENT TYPES OF CLUTTER: PHYSICAL, DIGITAL, ENERGETIC, MENTAL
3. CLEARING CLUTTER IS AN AMAZING CATALYST FOR CHANGE IN YOUR LIFE
4. THIS IS A LIFELONG PROCESS THAT YOU WILL COME TO LOOK FORWARD TO

NINE

BEYOND THE CHATTER

"All the noise, noise, noise, NOISE!"
— Grinch, *How the Grinch Stole Christmas!*

WHEN I WAS A YOUNG TEEN, my mother tried her best to persuade me to meditate. She said that quieting my mind would be of great benefit to my well being. But I was young. It felt boring. And I really couldn't see what the big deal was.

I dabbled with it occasionally, on and off, but not consistently like every day. And, when I did, all I would do is sit there and think. Thoughts would come to me, and it rarely ever felt like I was actually *quieting my mind*. I'm kind of embarrassed to say that I resisted daily meditation for nearly 15 years. I mean, that's a long time! The problem was that I really didn't understand the benefits of it.

Sure, I was told and read that the goal was to quiet the mind or focus one's attention, that it can help to reduce stress, but what did that really mean? I didn't feel any less stress. I could see the advantages of a regular meditation practice if I was maybe on an extended retreat or living the life of a monk or nun, but what did that have to do with my normal daily life? I just didn't feel like meditation in the traditional sense was for me.

Like I said, years passed. It wasn't until one day that a realization came to me and I finally understood the true benefit of meditation. The idea of quieting the mind is a bit of a misnomer. The goal is not to stop the chatter but rather to simply peer through it to the silence that is beyond. Noticing and allowing the gaps between the thoughts is all it takes to raise your vibration. And raising your vibration is what meditation is really all about. The higher your frequency, the more in line you are with your inner guidance and true self, and this is when your life truly begins to transform.

As your vibration rises with each meditation, you start to attract people, situations, and things into your life that are aligned with who you really are and what you want. Long-held negative feelings yield to higher vibe emotions. And yes, lower stress levels can be the result. Meditation opens your mind to understanding your life from a higher perspective, and it allows you to perceive connections and opportunities that you might have otherwise missed.

The What

Traditional meditation involves a focal point, something to direct your attention back to if your mind wanders. Focusing on your breathing is a very common practice, gently observing the rise and fall of each inhale and exhale. Listening to a sound is another powerful approach. Singing bowls, relaxing music, nature ambiance, or even the drone of a window fan can serve in this regard. Smells such as incense (make sure your space is well ventilated) or essential oil diffusers can also function in this capacity. It's really up to you and what feels best in the moment. Whatever you choose, you can use it as your focal point to which you'll gently turn your attention back to whenever you notice your thoughts going astray.

Again, a common misunderstanding people have about meditation is that they think the goal is to not think any thoughts during the session. But this is not necessary. If your head feels full, and all you're able to achieve are a few momentary lapses in your stream of thought, believe me, this is a successful meditation! How can this be? Because that's all it takes. A connection has occurred. A shift has begun. And because your meditation practice is a daily activity, the progress you make will build upon itself.

It's better to meditate for 15 minutes seven days in a row than to go for an hour only two or three times per week. The benefit comes from the consistency. Regular short, daily meditations will propel you forward on your path. After just a few sessions, you'll begin to notice improvement in diverse areas of your life. Just embrace the *knowing* that no matter what you experience during your meditation, behind the scenes, your vibration is on the rise. So relax, go with it, and enjoy whatever happens. And by the way, don't let the label, *meditation,* deter you from this practice. If you prefer a different name, such as, *centering*, *focusing*, or *quiet time*, then use that tag instead. Just do the practice.

And if you are wondering what time is the best for meditation, of course, that is up to each individual. However, an early morning session does set the tone for the rest of your day. So if you're up for it, I highly recommend meditating early, before the rest of your day gets started.

The How

- Set aside 15 minutes each day, ideally in the morning
- Find a comfortable spot, one where you won't be interrupted
- Sit or lay down (just don't fall asleep)
- Turn on a fan, air conditioner, or find a monotonous sound on a phone app
- Alternatively, you can focus on your breathing; follow your breath in and out.
- Set a timer for the allotted time (one with a peaceful alarm) and begin
- Take a deep breath in, then let it out; remember to keep breathing naturally
- Let your thoughts quiet down and drift away
- Focus on your sound or breath; if your attention wanders, gently bring it back

At the completion of your meditation, you may feel lighter, quieter, more relaxed. This is evidence that your vibration has risen. You had a successful session. However, it's also possible that you felt uncomfortable or even irritable. You may feel like, *I didn't get anything out of this. My mind was wandering too much. Thoughts kept popping in my head.* This is all part of the process. Even if you only had a brief instance of non-thought, it will prove to be very beneficial for you as you move forward.

Also, don't discount all those thoughts that came to

you. Take a moment to think about them because it's possible that some were actually coming from your inner guidance. How do you know? It's all in how they make you feel. If you feel good or even inspired by them, then they're coming from a higher vibration. If not, no worries. These will fade away the more regularly you meditate.

After you've achieved some consistency with your practice, feel free to experiment with additional methods if they appeal to you. These may include guided meditations, moving meditations (intuitive dance, tai chi, contemplative walking), reciting mantras (or affirmations), manipulation of the breath and more.

Daily meditation will reveal the state of your mind, where you're at on the emotional ladder. It will help you navigate and go beyond that voice of the ego (your monkey mind), allowing you to uncover your true guidance. Inner guidance is coming to you all the time. You will hear it through the gaps in your thoughts. Meditation is a vehicle that will help this happen more and more. It is the first step to allowing a whole lot more into your life.

TAKAWAYS - CHAPTER 9
BEYOND THE CHATTER

1. The goal of meditation is to connect with the silence beyond the chatter
2. The benefit of meditation is that it effectively raises your vibration
3. Consistency is key; short daily sessions are better the longer sporadic ones
4. Early morning is a great time to meditate; sets the tone for the day

TEN

POPPING THE BUBBLE

YOUR HEART KNOWS THE WAY. RUN IN THAT DIRECTION.
—RUMI

WE ALL HAVE a bubble of misinformation surrounding us. It begins to take shape when we are still quite young, when we learn (from mostly well-intentioned people) that we must believe in a dependency on others for our well-being.

According to universal principles, we create our own circumstances, our own reality. Yet, most of us are taught just the opposite, that we first must be dependent on our parents to provide for us. Then we are dependent on our employer or customers or clients for our livelihoods. We are dependent upon our neighbors and like-minded communities for security. We are dependent upon our spiritual leaders to contact the Divine for us, to intervene and interpret for us.

I call this *the bubble* because the idea of interdependency sounds good, even protective and comforting. However, it is a fallacy, and we are much better off without it. Let's pop this bubble of misinformation.

We are not dependent on anybody. Everything in our lives comes to us as a result of what we attract through our personal vibration. And I mean everything. You are the creator of your life. When you come to understand this, and take responsibility for it, everything changes. The way you view the world and how it works will be transformed.

Obviously a small child requires the basic necessities of life to be provided for by someone. What I'm saying is if this child maintains a high vibrational frequency, she will attract whatever she needs into her life. Although it may appear to be her parents doing the providing, it's the little girl's strength of vision in her own well-being that creates the comforting life she desires.

As newborns, we all came into this physical existence with the singular focus of joy and well-being. Clearly, not all of us were able to maintain that vision, but it doesn't mean we are forever barred from regaining it.

When circumstances and events occur in our lives that bring us serious discomfort, it's easy to question the law of universal magnetics. *I didn't create this! Why would I attract things I don't like?* We all come from different backgrounds. Everyone has their own path, some more challenging than others. Yet, no matter where we've been or where we find ourselves, if we're in situations we don't like, it's because, on some level, we are creating from a place of unawareness. Most of us haven't been taught how to direct our focus. So we end up reacting over and over to the world around us, rather than consciously creating the one we desire. With only a little tweaking, though, we can begin to turn things around.

What Brings You Joy?

The simplest way to begin attracting what you want is to practice feeling happy. Keep it simple, keep it real. Take a walk, pet a kitten, read a book, dance in your living room, meet up with good-feeling friends. Whatever it is you do, do it just for the fun of it. The Universe knows what you want. You just need to be in a place where you can receive it. The better you feel, the faster you'll attract it.

Once you find yourself resonating more and more in the higher emotional frequencies of contentment, positive expectation, and even passion, then begin to set intentions. Start your day with a positive statement such as, *Today is going to be an amazing day. I am safe, I am happy, and wonderful things are going to come my way.* Now watch for them to show up. And when they do, be sure to thank and acknowledge. If you appreciate something, your attention goes there, and you get more.

You Have Your Own Direct Connection

Another bubble worth popping is the idea that we need an intermediary between us and our higher being (source, force, god, or whatever you choose to call your spiritual origin). While it's sometimes nice to hear a different perspective or validation from other people, you are not dependent on anyone else to tell you what truth is for you.

We all have the ability to tap into our own higher guidance, on any subject at any time. It's how we are hardwired. We may think we're just physical bodies in a physical world; after all, this is what most of us are taught. But right here, right now, the greater part of us is alive and well in the non-physical realm. And it's through this non-physical connection that our inner guidance is always available to us.

So how do I connect? Quiet your mind. Impressions from your inner guidance slip in through the space between your thoughts. So the less you think, the more you receive. That's why introspective activities serve people so well. Meditate, walk in nature, listen to uplifting music, paint or draw or sculpt or dance or play. Find something that works for you.

As discussed in the previous chapter, even if you're new to meditation, it's not difficult. Really. Find a comfortable quiet location, sit or lie down, close your eyes, and take some deep breaths. Don't overthink it. Don't force it. The goal is not to stop your thoughts, but to simply soften them. Concentrate on your breathing or a steady sound in the room. Play some soothing music or listen to one of the many guided audio meditations that are available. Spend 15 minutes each day. Stick with it—even if you feel nothing is happening—because something is.

Inner guidance is coming to you at all times, but if you're not attuned to it, you'll miss the message. Don't beat yourself up over it. Your higher being won't ever stop trying to reach you. There's always another opportunity.

If you want to ask a question, state it before you meditate, then let it go. Don't expect an answer immediately. Sometimes one will come, but other times there's an intermission before the answer manifests. Ask, let go, then expect to receive.

The more consistent you are at quieting yourself during meditation (or other introspective practices), the greater your attunement will be with your non-physical self. You'll begin to pick up on the guidance that is coming to you all day, everyday.

Your inner guidance is clever. It will show up in a never-dull, never-ending variety of ways. A thought, word, or image that pops into your head. A synchronicity, a gut feeling, an intuition, something out of the ordinary occurs. The billboard advertisement along the highway, a song verse you hear playing in the grocery store, a smile from a young child, a double rainbow after a storm.

Is the message truly coming from your inner self? Or is it just your own overactive mind? Your clue is in how it strikes you, if it feels significant. Quite often, it might mean nothing to anyone else, but you notice it! It feels inspired. There's a moment of hopefulness, awe, or bliss. Is the message life-changing? Could be. But it doesn't have to be. Yet, it will always be uplifting in some way. The point is you are loved and non-physical has your back.

Animals As Messengers

Animals are often messengers in this regard, willing participants who come to play with us. In an example from just this morning, I was awakened early by the smell of diesel fumes coming into our bedroom window. Eew! This had never happened before. Robert and I live four flights up, and a garbage truck was picking up cans on the street below. It was shortly after daybreak, and I, still fighting to remain asleep, resisted getting up to close the window. However, my nasal passages started reacting to the diesel smell so my nose won out. I stumbled out of bed.

The blinds weren't entirely closed because I had a fan in the bottom of the window to draw in cool air at night. Today it was pulling in the diesel. As I wobbled half asleep over to the window, I could see outside around the fan. There—staring right at me—was a gorgeous hummingbird hovering in the air. Again, we are four stories up! It floated there, flitting slightly back and forth for a moment, then zoom! Away it went, back down towards the ground and on out of sight. This was a marvelous sign for me! How do I know?

Let's break it down. First, I was asleep. When we sleep, our linear minds turn off. We drop our resistance and enter a more pure state of being. I awoke suddenly and unexpectedly, which meant I was tired and not yet fully back into full normal waking consciousness. The diesel smell was unpleasant, but generally, I was still riding a good vibe from a pleasing night sleep.

Next, seeing a hummingbird four floors up, outside my window, in the city, was quite unusual. Out of the ordinary. We don't have any flowers or plants outside the window to attract a hummer. We've lived at this location for over six years. Never once have I seen a hummingbird anywhere near our building.

Finally, as I already mentioned, I love hummingbirds, always have since childhood. I consider them to be one of my favorite animals. I've had many joyful experiences with hummers in the past, and they hold a special place in my heart.

So yes, this was guidance coming to me. Sometimes we know immediately what the communication means. Other times, you may need to check-in with yourself, meditate on it, or simply allow the meaning to come to you when you're not trying so hard to figure it out.

What did this particular hummer sign mean for me? It was a reminder that all is going well in my life. Everything is happening when it should, and things that may seem dark or unpleasant at times, are nothing more than a way for me to refine what I want in my life. It was gentle prompt to continue to focus on the things that bring me joy.

If you want to go further, I created an online course, *Popping the Bubble: How to Connect to Your Universal Guidance in 7 Days or Less*. Find it at:

https://tashaiarts.samcart.com/products/popping-the-bubble-workshop

TAKEAWAY - CHAPTER 10
POPPING THE BUBBLE

~

1. MOST OF US HAVE A BUBBLE OF MISINFORMATION AROUND US
2. WE ARE NOT DEPENDENT ON ANYONE; WE CREATE OUR OWN REALITY
3. AS YOUR VIBRATION RISES, SET INTENTIONS FOR YOUR DAY
4. DAILY MEDITATION (OR ANOTHER INTROSPECTIVE PRACTICE) PROVIDES A FOUNDATION FOR QUIETING YOUR MIND AND OPENING YOU UP TO YOUR INNER GUIDANCE
5. GUIDANCE (OR SIGNS) ARE ALL AROUND; IF YOU LOOK, YOU'LL NOTICE THEM

ELEVEN

THE MENTAL SIDE OF LETTING GO

> In the process of letting go, you will lose many things from the past, but you will find yourself.
> —Deepak Chopra

As you probably gathered from the very first chapter in this book, I am not a fan of looking back. Sure, basking in the warm glow of a fond memory, that's wonderful—especially if it's part of a daily routine of focusing on things that bring you joy. Past, present, future—the *when* of your happy thoughts doesn't matter.

However, the practice of digging up old emotional wounds did no favors for my mother. She found no catharsis in rehashing the painful events from her early life. All she really achieved was to take up residence at the bottom end of the emotional spectrum.

If you are seeking to improve your life in some way, to reach a desired goal, then dredging up a grievous past event is like taking a detour through a construction zone rather than staying on the fast-moving freeway. I'm a strong proponent of looking for something to feel good about now. Anything from your past that is still carrying an antagonistic emotional charge for you today is only doing so because you continue to think about it in the present. Changing your focus in the here and now fills your life with new now thoughts, new now actions and a new now vibrational countenance.

However, if you find your attempts at thinking happier thoughts being sabotaged by painful memories, then there are a couple of techniques that can help you get over the hump, so to speak. These practices will enable you to raise your emotional frequency to a new median, allowing you to direct your thoughts upwards more easily.

Forgiveness

Substantial scientific evidence exists on the healing impact of forgiveness. For decades, researchers have been conducting studies with findings that highlight the importance of letting go of grievances that no longer serve us. The correlation between the act of forgiving and improved mental and physiological health is real. The list of positive benefits is extensive. This is common sense, right? If it doesn't serve us, let that shit go. But how?

How do we forgive someone who we perceive has hurt us? Forgiveness is not about right or wrong. When we forgive another, we are not saying what they did was okay. In fact, the process of forgiveness isn't really about the other party at all. It's for our own well-being, for us to regain our energetic vitality that is currently being consumed by our attention to what others said or did.

If you've read this far in the book, then you

understand the law of attraction. You know that your emotional state is a reflection of the things you give your attention to. This is not a judgment, you are not right or wrong for how you are feeling. It's simply where you are in any given moment. You, and you alone, have the power to change how you're really feeling. Isn't this good to know? Most of the world is busy blaming others for this or that. But you understand that what's *out there* doesn't have to affect you. Only you control your destiny. With this in mind, let's raise your vibration and get forgiveness working for you.

A simple yet effective forgiveness method is one you may have already heard of, Ho'oponopono (pronounced *HO-oh-Po-no-Po-no*). This ritual, performed by traditional Hawaiian healers, has grown in popularity in recent years and has been adopted by many. It includes a mantra of sorts, four lines aimed at restoring balance in one's life through forgiveness—particularly forgiveness of self.

The traditional lines are said in this order: *I'm sorry. Please forgive me, Thank you. I love you.* The second line often confuses people because, *Please forgive me*, doesn't seem to fit if you are thinking about how you were hurt by another. However, the traditional Hawaiian healers understand that no matter who or what we may think is to blame, self-forgiveness is needed to move on.

I have found that a slight adaptation of the lines seems to work best for me personally. If true healing is the goal here, you should do what resonates most with you. This is what I say and usually in this order, although I will also shuffle that too if it feels right at the time: *I'm sorry. I forgive you. I love you. Thank you.*

We came to this world to learn, grow and have fun in our lives. Being human and making human mistakes is all a part of that experience. Yet, we're often way too hard on ourselves for not being perfect.

On some level, we know who we truly are. Our non-physical aspect—our inner beings—are pure love, freedom, joy, and empowerment. And as as difficult as it may sometimes be to believe or even comprehend, this is also who we really are right here in the physical world. Any thought to the contrary is the cause of pain, both emotional and physical.

This is why self-forgiveness is so important. It's about forgiving ourselves for not living up to these standards, for beating up on ourselves for not being perfect. It's about forgiving ourselves for not remembering who we really are.

The Ho'oponopono technique is simple, and setting an intention of self-forgiveness before you start will be of great benefit. Think about a past incident that still holds a negative emotional charge for you, whether it's something someone did to you or you did to them. Feel the feeling that comes up. Now recite the series of four statements. Take your time. Breath. Feel a release.

Forgivness Technique

I'm sorry. Whether you're the perceived victim or transgressor, your intention is, *I'm sorry for thinking less of myself. I am more than this, I am pure love.* And if there is a victimizer, *I am sorry for thinking less of you. You are more than this too.*

I forgive you. Victim or transgressor, in either case, you are talking to yourself. Of course, you also intend forgiveness for the victimizer here when there is one.

. . .

I love you. *I love myself, my inner being, and you* (the victimizer). *I know that your true self is also pure love, and you acted the way you did because you were feeling disconnected from who you really are too.*

Thank you. The intention is meant for self and victimizer. *Thank you for helping me see this about myself.*

Repeat the lines as often as is necessary. Now let it go.

This practice is not complicated, yet it works exceeding well. Set your intentions, practice forgiveness, and feel your emotional frequency rise to a level where it no longer resonates with guilt or the victim mentality. Thoughts of the transgression will no longer hold an emotional charge. It's the true meaning of *forgive and forget.*

Tapping

Sometimes you feel stuck, emotionally stagnant. You're not. You can't be, it's not possible. Who you truly are is vibrant and always expanding. Nonetheless, there are times when it feels like you're just circling the drain. When this happens, there's another exercise you can employ which will restore a sense of balance in your life.

Back in 2013, a friend introduced me to the Emotional Freedom Technique (EFT), and I've been using it ever since. Also called *tapping*, this practice was developed in the mid

1990s by Gary Craig. Based on the Chinese medicine concept of meridian points found throughout the body, EFT helps clear energetic/emotional blockages, allowing our natural chi (or vital life force) to flow, similar to the way that acupuncture and acupressure work.

The technique is easy to learn and involves using your hand to tap meridian points on your head and upper body as you focus on the issue you want to clear, whether it be mental or physical.

Start by identifying an issue and stating it out loud. Focus on just one issue at a time to keep it simple. For example, *I'm worried about what other people think of me*. You might also add the why, *...because I feel inferior.* If there is a physical sensation, you can include this too, *...and I feel a tightness in my jaw because of this.* The most effective time to tap is when you feel the problem, when it's in your face. You want the emotions raw and ready. So be sure to *feel* it.

Now, make a statement out loud again, this time as a proclamation of your acceptance of yourself in spite of this issue. And add a final declaration about loving and accepting yourself. *Even though I am worried about what other people think about me because I feel inferior and it's causing a tightness in my jaw, I deeply and completely love and accept myself.*

Begin tapping with two or three fingers of one hand (doesn't matter which) on the *karate chop* side of your other hand. Be gentle but firm. Repeat the proclamation statement out loud five or more times. As you do this, deeper or more uncomfortable feelings may start to rise to the surface, fears, feelings of unworthiness. For example, you may realize that your mother was overly critical of you when you were young. When these start to appear, say them out loud and switch to the following tapping sequence for the remainder of the session.

Tapping Sequence Points

- Inside eyebrow
- Outside eyebrow, side of eye
- Under the eye
- Under the nose
- Chin
- Inner collarbone
- Under the arm
- Top of the head

As you move through the eight-point sequence, say reminder phrases to keep your focus on why you are tapping. In our example, you might state something like, *The fear of people judging me.* Or *The worry about being criticized or rejected.* And, *I feel inferior to others.* Bringing attention to these feelings allows you to release them.

After running through the sequence another time or two, the intensity of these emotions will soften. This is when you can add more positive affirmations like, *I am now releasing all of this worry. Feelings of fear are clearing from the cells of my body. Tension is leaving my jaw.* Continue on until you you truly feel some level of relief. Before you stop, anchor in a positive statement of change to replace that other feeling. Something like, *I am a strong, confident being of light. I deeply and completely love and accept myself.*

Using this example above, I created an introduction video, *How to Tap*, just for readers of this book. Sign up at https://www.tashai.net/pages/get-free-stuff44637   and you'll get instant access.

When you feel you are done, take a deep breath. Note how intense the emotions were at the beginning of the session and compare them to how you are now. If you don't feel like you achieved much relief, go through the process again, but adjust your proclamation phrase to reflect more closely the emotions you have now. No matter what, you will have taken a step towards raising your vibrational frequency and clearing out some old beliefs. Congratulations!

If you find yourself having difficulty focusing on happier things, then use one or both of the techniques discussed in this chapter to breakthrough. Forgiveness and tapping are tools to help you clear old limiting thoughts that, quite possibly, have been lingering unnoticed for god-knows-how-long. The release allows you to think kinder, more loving thoughts about yourself and others. This, in turn, brings you more into alignment with your true self. Use these tools often. They will allow you to reach new levels in your relationships, your finances, or whatever it is that's calling you forward.

TAKEAWAYS - CHAPTER 11
THE MENTAL SIDE OF LETTING GO

1. IF PAINFUL MEMORIES ARE SABOTAGING YOUR HAPPY THOUGHTS, THERE ARE TECHNIQUES YOU CAN DO TO CHANGE THIS
2. INTEND SELF-FORGIVENESS
3. FORGIVENESS EXERCISE (HO'OPONOPONO)
4. YOUR THOUGHTS AND EMOTIONS ARE NOT "STUCK"
5. TAPPING EXERCISE (EFT)

TWELVE

TRUST THE UNIVERSE

FOLLOW YOUR BLISS! Joseph Campbell's well-known manifesto has been a personal mantra of mine throughout my life. From firsthand experience, I know it to be true. *The universe will open doors for you where there were only walls.*

Still. This doesn't mean you won't ever experience circumstances that suck. You don't become immune to what some call failure. There are times when things just don't seem to work out. What you can count on, however, is the universe being there for you, always, unfailingly, bringing you what *you* think you deserve. You're the one calling the shots. You get as much good as you want in direct proportion to how much your vibrational frequency can tolerate it. So if you truly are following your bliss, and that truly is your focus, rather than on the fear of failure or other worries, then prepare yourself for the life of your dreams!

You are not being tested, punished, forgotten, or abandoned. You don't have to pay your dues or wait your turn. You are alive here in the physical. You have the support of the greater part of yourself which resides in non-physical. And the whole universe has your back. That's how much you are loved. That's how important you are. If you have a desire, if you feel a calling, then someway somehow you can reach it.

Remember the gap? It's that discrepancy between the vibration you are currently resonating with and the one you would have if you were living the life of your dreams. You've done the prep work. The foundation is in place for your bridge. Maybe you've honed your focus; or you've become a meditator and have worked your way up the emotional ladder; it's possible you found alignment through a connection with nature or by decluttering your life; you tuned into inner guidance, did forgiveness work, or practiced the tapping technique.

So where the hell is the life of my dreams? you ask. *I'm not living it yet!* Are you sure? Maybe you are more than you realize. These changes can be subtle. Something better here, an upgrade there. This is in direct response to whatever vibration you are putting out. There's also a lot of behind-the-scenes rearranging going on, setting up situations, laying the groundwork for your new life.

If you are continually focusing on *not having* what you want, then you're out of sync with the vibrational frequency of *having* it. There comes a point where you simply need to let go, metaphorically step out over the edge and trust that your bridge will spring into concreteness underfoot. Trust that the universe has your back every moment of everyday. Trust.

You might call it having faith. I don't particularly dig this word, *faith*, not only because of the religious connotations, but it also somehow implies that we should believe in something without any proof. In fact, one of the definitions found in the Merriam-Webster dictionary says as much: *a firm belief in something for which there is no proof.* Don't get me wrong, If you have a firm belief in something, even when there is no evidence to support it, you will manifest it into your life—if your desire and focus is true and unwavering.

The reason I prefer the word, *trust*, is that it implies a slightly different meaning, one that leans in the direction of *knowing*. Among the many perks that come from maintaining a higher emotional frequency is a sense of knowing. Belief transforms into knowing. Everything is working out for you even if you can't see it right now.

When my hubby and I lived in Colorado, we were seriously considering buying a motorcycle so the two of us could go for fun rides up in the mountains. Robert used to own a small 125cc dirt bike in his early teens, and although he hadn't ridden in years, he was quite confident that it would all come back to him once he was in the saddle again. We both wanted to be able to drive it so we signed up together for a motorcycle training course. It was held in the wide open parking lot of the then recently-closed and unused Stapleton International Airport in Denver. The class went well, we received our driver license certification, and started looking for a bike. Yet, things didn't materialize. Life got busy, other pursuits demanded attention, and then my mother became sick. We moved to the Midwest sans a motorcycle.

Fast-forward nearly 20 years later. I was a different person and hadn't thought about owning a motorcycle since forever. It wasn't even on my radar until I began to notice little inner nudges. At first, they were subtle, a pleasant feeling, an inspired thought. I'd imagine what it would be like out on the open road. Wind in my face. I took more notice of bikes when driving in my car. A friend casually brought up a conversation about Harleys. All this didn't necessarily mean I was *supposed* to get a motorcycle, but it did reawaken the idea. When I first told Robert this, his response was unenthusiastic. He said he really wasn't into them anymore. We laugh about this today because he now has more passion for riding than I. But at the time, I just let him think whatever he wanted. We'd been together long enough that he knew I was going to pursue my interests no mater what he thought. So I dove into my motorcycle research.

It wasn't long before things came into focus. I narrowed down my search to a Honda CTX700. I found one online. A late-model bike with super low miles. It was practically brand new. And being a cruiser-style, it looked cool too. This also meant, however, that it was slightly heavier than one that a beginner like myself might normally start out on. The bike dealer was located in Illinois, two and a half hours away (via highway). Synchronistically, we were already planning to be in Chicago the upcoming weekend to attend a workshop. I told Robert that afterwards, I wanted to go check out this bike. What he didn't know was that, if I liked it in person, I was going to put a down payment on it.

Flying high after the seminar, we walked into the

motorcycle showroom, and I knew immediately when I saw it. There was no wavering, no inner questioning. This was my bike. I started it up and it purred. But we couldn't actually take it for a test ride. The cycle classification that both Robert and I obtained in Colorado had transferred to our new driver licenses when we moved out of state, but during the numerous renewals over the past two decades, the motorcycle certification had somehow slipped through the cracks and no longer appeared on either of our actual licenses. We'd need to retake the driver's test to make it legal. Due to liability issues, the dealership understandably wasn't going to allow us to test drive the bike that day. I didn't need to. I *knew* this was the right thing to do. So I put the down payment on it, much to Robert's surprise.

That week, we visited the DMV, took a written test, and received temporary driving permits. We could now legally ride the bike home, and then practice with it before retaking the driving portion of the test at a later date. The dealership said they would hold my Honda for one week. We were set to pick it up on Saturday. Because Robert had had so much more experience on a motorcycle than me, we decided he should drive it home from the dealer and I would follow behind in the car. Unbeknownst to me, a sense of apprehension was slowly growing in him concerning the ride. Sure, he did have a motorcycle when he was a kid but that was over 40 years ago. Also that machine was just a small dirt bike that he never drove on-road, especially in amongst traffic. Without mentioning anything to me, he started checking the weather app on his phone for northern Illinois.

As each day passed, my excitement grew, so did his anxiety. Robert began vocalizing some of his concerns. He especially wanted me to look at that weather app. I said, *No thanks. Everything is going to work out fine.* And I meant it. I felt it. I just knew it. One day to go. He tried again with the app, but I refused. It is with *knowing* that you create your life. I wasn't going to let any outside influences affect what I knew to be true. He tried bargaining with me, suggesting we contact the dealership to choose another day for pick-up. Yet, even he knew this wouldn't be feasible with his own work schedule and the dealership being closed on Sundays. It was now or never.

We woke to overcast skies. As we got ready, I saw Robert looking at his phone. I reminded him that it will all work out fine. *It's going to be a fun day!* He didn't share my enthusiasm. When we got there, the dealership had the bike prepped and ready. I paid the remainder of the bill, they rolled the Honda out into the side parking lot, we shook hands, and the deal was done. There we were, just Robert and me standing next to the bike. I started it up while he put on his helmet and gloves. He climbed on and the first few drops of rain began to fall. I suggested he do a couple loops around the parking lot to get a feel for it. He did. This was definitely a heavier bike than what he was used to. Watching him, I must admit that I had a momentary concern. It's understandable that he would be a bit rusty, but he looked it. Yet, dark clouds were upon us, the rain was picking up, and there was no time to waste. We needed to go.

It was decided that I would lead the way in my car so he wouldn't have to worry about navigating our route home. We would be taking back country roads as much as possible, but we'd still need to pass through a number of small cities with plenty of traffic. Minutes into the ride, the skies opened and Robert was getting drenched in the downpour. We drove for about 20 minutes in the rain until coming to a town with a Walgreens. We pulled into the parking lot, and he hopped in the passenger seat of my car to get a reprieve from the storm. It was really coming down now, with a couple of lightning flashes thrown in for dramatic effect as well. For someone who had never driven in traffic and in a downpour, he was doing alright. I could see he was still nervous, but there was also another part of him emerging. He was wide-eyed and excited. This was an adventure. We planned out the next stretch of road, then continued on.

From that point on, the rain began to lighten. Another 10 minutes, it turned to a drizzle, then subsided altogether. The roads where still wet, but it wasn't long before the clouds started to break up with the sun poking through. An hour into the drive, I pulled off to the side of the road near an open field to take a break. The clouds had dispersed, the sun was fully out, and the roads were drying. We rested and ate. Robert was a different person now. He said it was all coming back to him, he was no longer afraid but instead was having fun. I was ecstatic to hear this.

He took the lead from there, and when we finally arrived back in our home town, we stopped at our favorite restaurant to celebrate. He admitted to me just how terrified he had been at the outset. He hadn't felt fear like that since he was a child. We both laughed. Don't get me wrong. I would never have asked Robert to do anything dangerous. I knew he could do it. He was just nervous. But it was also something he wanted to do. In fact, for him, it was sort of a trial by fire (or in this case, water). And he came out the other side a new person. To this day, he has no fear about taking our big Kawasaki Vulcan 1700cc out on the streets during a rainstorm. There could not have been a better baptism back into the world of riding than this.

When we returned home, he showed me the radar map he'd saved on his phone from the morning. I could now understand why he was so apprehensive. It showed a huge mass of thunderstorms covering the entire route we took back home. It was supposed to be an all day assault with no signs of letting up until evening. Yet, in our reality, it only really lasted about a half hour then petered out. *You changed the weather,* he said. I responded, *Because I never doubted. We were meant to do this today. I knew everything would work out fine.* That's the power of knowing. When you are totally committed boobs to bones, the universe will co-conspire with you. Belief is one thing, but when you *know*, you're in the high country.

As your trust in the universe grows, so will the manifestations of your desires. As they say, *The proof is in the pudding.* Your job is to relax and let yourself receive it. If you want something, then you've already attracted it to you on an energetic level. It's now searching for ways to materialize into your physical existence. Don't get in the way of it. Permit it to come by raising your vibration to meet it.

Look around right here, right now. You will see aspects of your dream life everywhere. Notice them, acknowledge them, and build your trust in the universe to bring what you've created.

Sure, there may be points in your life where you've come to a crossroads, where the way you are currently living is no longer sustainable, but at the same time, you don't know how you're going to move forward. You could worry about the situation. Or let go and trust.

Think of it this way. You are driving in your car on a straight road. On either side is a steep canyon wall. Up ahead is a bend in the road, but you can't see beyond that point. Yet, you're pretty damn sure the road continues. What do you do? Do you stop your car now before you reach the turn? Do you get out, pace back and forth, and worry about whether the road will go on? Do you wait, hoping for another car to come from the other direction to let you know if the road is safe? Of course not. You just continue driving on, going into the turn and picking up with the road beyond. It is really that easy.

You may not think this applies because what you're up against is so much larger, uncertain, and in your face than this simple analogy. I don't mean to make light of your particular situation, but if you're able to cultivate even a little trust in the universe, you will see results. The road beyond is already waiting for you. Just move in that direction, in the direction of your bliss.

TAKEAWAYS - CHAPTER 12
TRUST THE UNIVERSE

1. You attract what *you* think you deserve
2. The universe has your back
3. Trust leads to knowing
4. Relax and permit it to come to you
5. Keep going, the road is already waiting for you

THIRTEEN

NOW LET'S ACTUALLY CHANGE YOUR LIFE

You cannot get sick enough to help sick people get better. You cannot get poor enough to help poor people thrive. It is only in your thriving that you have anything to offer anyone. If you're wanting to be of an advantage to others, be as tapped in, tuned in, turned on as you can possibly be.

—Abraham-Hicks

Does the title of this chapter bring up any emotions for you? Any tingles, goosebumps, or even a release of a few tears? Or maybe just a feeling of hopefulness? If so, good, that means you're ready. Don't worry if you didn't experience anything like that because if you've come this far, then you're ready for change in your life too. You've made it almost to the end of this book which means something is calling you forward. If what you've been doing hasn't been working and your life isn't what you want it to be, then try something different. Right?

Motivation, however, will only get you so far. Ever have a New Year's resolution that you were so excited about, but then a few weeks later you'd forgotten all about it? Yeah, we all have. That's because while being motivated is great and it's what gets you started, it's not the sustaining part of the puzzle. What comes next is a change in habits. It's your day-to-day behaviors that will make or break your success.

So start now. Now is your time. You have tools to work with. All that is needed is to develop new patterns for your better life, and I'm going to help you do that. Studies have shown that it takes at least 21 days and up to three months for a new habit to form (or to break an old one). The length of time is dependent not just on your motivation, but also on how well you've integrated your new behavior into your life, plus the efficacy of the rewards you receive from this change.

The start of your day sets the tone for all that follows. Ever have a great morning and the rest of the day only gets better and better? The reverse, of course, is also true. Have a rough start and things just seem to go downhill from there. I'm not saying it's always this way. You certainly can turn your trajectory around. It just may take more effort.

When I was trying to change and improve my life organically, I didn't have a direct path laid out for me. I discovered numerous techniques that felt beneficial, but I wasn't clear on how to integrate them into my everyday routine. I was feeling a bit lost, like I was in a dense jungle. I had my machete in hand for clearing a path, but at the same time, I was blindfolded. I could cut an opening, take a step, but then I'd have to wait to see if this was actually the direction my inner being was calling me towards. I made progress, but it was slow. That's why I have included a roadmap for you in the form of a 30-day challenge.

From my personal experience and those of my coaching clients, I've found that a timeframe of 30 days seems to be the typical success number for most people. It takes about 30 days to implement a new behavior or release an old habit—as long as there is a solid strategy and action plan in place. So I have created a 30-day challenge for you, one that can change your life.

"When am I supposed to do this? I already have no time in my day!"

You may feel like you have no time to introduce anything new into your busy day. Trust me. I do understand. I've been there myself. Over the years, I have experienced many shifts and periods of growth in my life. However, there were two distinct times of change that propelled me forward more than anything else.

The Emotional Epiphany

The first one was an epiphany (as I mentioned in Chapter 5), the understanding that jumping from a low vibrational emotion like despair to the higher realm of bliss usually involves a multi-step process. Take the step that's in front of you. The embodiment of this realization permitted me to make huge strides forward. It allowed me to unstick myself and raise the emotional place where I was consistently hanging out, step by step.

The Action

The second change in my life was an action, one that I made a conscious decision to take. When I was in my teens, up until the time I graduated from high school, I would sleep at my grandparents house every other weekend as part of my father's custody agreement (he lived with my grandparents). I always loved to stay up late on nights when I didn't have to get up for school the next day. I was not a morning person. So on the weekends, I would roll out of bed at 11:00-11:30 am and stumble out into my grandparents kitchen. By this time, my grandfather would already be in the kitchen ready for his lunch. As soon as I set foot on the tile floor, he would cry out, *The dead has risen!* He'd laugh at his own joke, as if it was something new that he didn't say every single time I stayed there.

Everyone knew I was a confirmed night person, after high school, after college, after I was married, I still liked staying up late and getting up later. That was until I needed to do something more to change my life, something different. The problem was time, there was no time left in my day to do anything productive towards my goals. I worked all day and was just too drained in the evening. I tried but nothing seemed to work.

What if I could wake up earlier? I thought. *Hold on!,* some part of me protested. *I'm a night person!* But this belief about myself no longer mattered. My desire to change my life was so strong, I was willing to risk some discomfort. So I set my alarm 60 minutes early.

For the next five days, I woke up a hour early and partook in my morning practices (which I will explain in the 30-day challenge later in this chapter). I was feeling great about myself and my progress, but it still wasn't enough. So I set my alarm for another 60 minutes back. Now I was waking up everyday a full two hours early (don't worry, you won't have to do this). This simple but profound shift in my waking schedule made all the difference. I was so inspired by my life now. I could do all my self-improvement practices in the morning and then go to work. If I was drained at night and watched a little TV before bed, it didn't matter because I had already accomplished what I wanted to do that day. I felt renewed and like I was truly moving forward again.

The Morning

In the morning you are fresh into the world. Your optimism is high, your creativity is prepped and ready, and your willpower is at its highest for the day. This is the perfect time.

It didn't take me all that long to acclimate to my new morning schedule. I felt so inspired and encouraged by the progress I was making with my self-improvement goals that I was able to write an entire book while still holding down a 50 hour per week job. I had tried to write in the evenings, but I was so wiped from the workday, I had nothing creative left. But the mornings were a different story.

That's me. So why do I care about *your* progress? Because I've made it my mission to help as many people as I can to find their own success. I'm paying it forward for all the help I received from the teachers who came before me. In addition, every person that has success in creating the life of their dreams raises the vibration for everyone else here on the planet, which in turn, makes it possible for us all to reach new amazing expanded levels of living. So it's in my best interest, and everyone else's here with us, to help you reach the success you crave.

What Might You Expect From the 30-Day Challenge?

Take a deep breath. You guessed it. I'm going to challenge you to wake up earlier, just one hour earlier, for the next 30 days. If you're similar to most people, you'll probably go through four distinct stages during the challenge, each lasting about a week. You will confront a different set of mental and emotional speed bumps—the Big Bad Wolf aspect of your psyche—that may try to stop you from taking any further uncomfortable action. If you are prepared for these psychological hiccups and know they are a normal part of creating new life habits, you won't be derailed if something comes up for you. You'll have the foreknowledge and tools to overcome it.

Days 1-7 Phase One - The Little Death

The first few days might feel amazing. Why? Because it's fresh, exciting. You are taking action towards new success. You're experiencing a hopeful high! Soon, however, the newness wears off and your excitement may wane. It's common for your inner critical voice to awaken, and for you then to begin to hate this process. *It's the most stupid thing in the world and why am I even doing it?* This first phase can be a bit uncomfortable because it's causing a disruption in your old familiar routine. Did I mention you could hate it?

Don't worry! Know this. These feelings are temporary. This is not the way it will always feel. It's just the process of cutting a new path through the jungle of your habitual behaviors. It will take some time, but not too long before you will get that path cleared. This is the most challenging timeframe. This new habit won't always feel as it does right now. So don't stop. Ride the wave. It *will* get easier. Really!

Days 8-14 Phase Two - I'm Not Dying

During the second phase, things will lighten up. You may experience a few subtle dividends and successes coming to you as well as a little boost of self-confidence. You will still need to discipline yourself and stay committed. There could be some lingering discomfort of change, but it will be less than in the previous stage. Remember, just because you don't yet see all the progress being made behind the scenes, doesn't mean it's not starting to materialize all around you. Look with new eyes. Find those things that resonate with who you are. Acknowledge and appreciate. The joy you seek is here right now. When you're cognizant of what has already come your way, you open an avenue for the universe to bring you more.

Days 15-21 Phase Three - Step Off the Carousel

Like a horse glimpsing freedom and stepping off the carousel for the first time, you are beginning to feel a whole lot better about yourself in this third phase. You are doing well. The goal here is to not to spook yourself. We don't want you running for the cover of familiar but old undesirable habits. You'll probably be feeling pretty good about how much you've accomplished so far. Just look at your progress! You're creating new habits, but are they yet sustainable? Stick with it. You are in the process of becoming. You want your new behaviors to metamorphose into a long term personal paradigm.

Days 21-30 Phase Four - I Am a Badass

At this stage, you may feel like you've made it. The danger, if there is one, is simply one of over-confidence. You've come so far that you feel like a god or goddess. You may even think you can take a fews days off. Don't. This is where you really start seeing and enjoying the fruits of your previous 20 days of labor. Any joy that you feel during this time will make it possible for you to turn this challenge into a lifetime of success. If you take a break from your new habits before you've reached the 30-day positive reinforcement point, it could be a hard sell getting back on the horse. So stick with it baby!

A Life of Ease

As I mentioned back in the introduction to this book, effort and struggle are not a prerequisite for manifesting the life you want. Using these simple but effective techniques can open you up to a world of wonderment. It doesn't have to be difficult. However, you do have to align with it, with the life you desire. If what you are reaching for seems like a struggle, tone it down. Start at a place that feels comfortable, something you can sincerely resonate with. Then go from there.

What does it really mean when someone says to you, *If you want to change your life, just do the work.* Not sure? This is what the 30-day challenge is all about. It's your blueprint for how you can begin to implement the practices in this book. Start filling in that gap between where you are now and the life of your dreams. Take my 30-day challenge.

The Fill the Gap and Shine 30-Day Life Transformation Challenge

The purpose of the 30-day challenge is to give you a road map, a route that leads to new habits. It will awaken in you who you really are—the kind of person who actually attracts the life you want (rather than one who thinks it could never happen for you). It's called *Fill The Gap and Shine* because we all rise everyday, but how many of us really shine? *This* will put that shine back into your morning!

I AM Morning

To fit this new adventure into your current life, you will wake up at least one hour earlier than normal in order to partake in these life-changing practices. If you start your morning on a high note—a higher frequency—you will begin to see this high vibe sticking with you progressively longer and longer throughout each day. Your self-esteem will rise, and you will feel better and better about yourself as the days go by. You will likely start to receive clearer guidance and ideas from your inner-self in regards to what steps you can take next towards reaching your goals.

To change your life, you need to upgrade yourself. These three *I AM* morning practices will help you to do just that.

Invigorate. Annotate. Meditate. When you wake in the morning, this is your itinerary to start the day:

- Invigorate (exercise) for 20 minutes
- Annotate (journal) for 15 minutes
- Meditate (connect) for 15 minutes

~

This leaves you 10 minutes to spare. Choose one of the following practices to fill out your hour.

- Affirmations
- Tapping
- Visualization

Do one of these per session, but feel free to rotate with the others on subsequent days. In other words, choose the one (affirmations, tapping or visualization) that you feel will serve you best on any particular day.

The Nitty Gritty

Invigorate - 20 minutes

Get your blood flowing. Generate some kinetic energy. During this first segment, you'll move your body. Do some form of exercise: walk, run, get on the elliptical or stationary bike, bounce on the rebounder, lift weights, do yoga postures. Find workouts which fit into this time frame and ones that appeal to you. Go at your own pace, and if this is new to you, ease into it. Mix it up too. Changing up your routines on different days will help keep it fresh and will also work different muscles. Be sure to get anything you may need for your workout ready the night before, so there are no excuses not to follow through.

Annotate - 15 minutes

The purpose of this second segment is to clear your head, frankly, to do a brain dump. Get yourself a notebook and write. But there is no specific topic for this kind of journaling. Just write whatever is on your mind, dump it onto the page. Don't worry about sentence structure or grammar, whether it makes sense or not. Dump. You are releasing and opening up space. After a time of doing this, you may find that on some days, insights will come to you. Ideas that might have otherwise escaped your notice will conveniently become clear. Your writing may transform from random thoughts into inspiring messages and exciting new goals. But don't try to make anything happen. Just write whatever comes to you no matter what it is. The goal is to dump.

Meditate - 15 minutes

Relax quietly without outside distraction. Meditation is as varied as individuals are. In the beginning, it may help to listen to an audio guided meditation. Or you can focus on a sound, follow your breathing, lay on your back, sit in a chair, or relax in a resting yoga pose. Whatever form of meditation you choose, the purpose here is to connect with your inner self. This is accomplished by releasing stress and calming the mind. This in turn raises your vibration. Whenever your mind wanders, gently and kindly bring it back to your focal point. Even if you're only able to quiet your mental activity for a brief moment during this time, this will have a sincere impact on the rest of your day. It truly doesn't take much to effect real change.

Look back at chapter 9 to refresh your memory on how

to get started with meditation or check out my course, *Popping The Bubble: How to Connect With Your Inner Guidance in 7 Days or Less,* https://tashaiarts.samcart.com/products/popping-the-bubble-workshop

Tapping, Affirmations or Visualization. "How do I know which to choose?"

Tapping

If when you awaken you realize that you were having nightmares or you are feeling anxiety, fear, anger or general uneasiness, then tapping is a good choice. (See the tapping techniques from Chapter 10 to refresh your memory on how to do this.) It's really quite simple once you start, but don't be fooled, this is a powerful practice that will bring you relief from negative patterns.

Affirmations

Are you working toward a specific goal? Looking for a new home? Wanting to double your income in the next six months? Doesn't matter what the objective is, using a set of positive affirmations that reflect this goal can be a powerful tool in your kit. Write your affirmations down, keep the focus on the positive, read them, say them out loud while staring into a mirror. You are training yourself to come into sync with your intention. When you do, the universe has to bring it to you. That's how the law of attraction works.

However, there is a secret to affirmations that hardly anyone ever mentions. In regards to the subject matter of your affirmation, you have to feel that it is actually possible.

You have to believe it can be true for you. If you don't, if you have doubts or feelings of unworthiness, then something else is occurring. What you are affirming then are these limiting beliefs. It's not so much the words that count, but the feelings behind them. So begin by making affirmations you can truly believe in. If, for example, you have trouble saying that you love yourself. You can try something less controversial such as, *I'm learning to love myself.* The point is, create your affirmations in a way that you feel the truth in them for you. Don't try to force yourself to feel something that doesn't yet resonate. As you progress, your beliefs will change and expand, your vibration will rise, and then you can shoot for the stars.

New to affirmations? Get some examples by listening to my audio, *Raise Your Vibration Affirmations.* Find it on the *Fill the Gap* book extras:

https://www.tashai.net/pages/get-free-stuff44637

Visualization

Let's say you have a work presentation coming up and you need it to go well, but you're nervous about how you'll do. Use the power of your mind to visualize the outcome you want. See it in as much detail as you can. The subconscious doesn't know if you are really experiencing it or if you are just picturing it in your mind's eye. Use this hack to your advantage to mentally picture the positive outcome you desire.

Boost your visualizing with a vision board. A vision board is a visual aid which helps you picture your goals and desires more clearly. It can be an actual physical board, like a bulletin board, filled with photos, magazine clippings, drawings, etc. Or it can be in a digital format, such as a private Instagram or Pinterest account to which you can add photos that you find on the internet. When you look at the images, feel the good feelings that arise in you. You are attuning to them.

30-days and Beyond

Wash, rinse, and repeat. For the next 30-days, commit yourself to these practices. You will see amazing results. After a month of this, these life enhancing habits will become integrated and will feel a natural part of your life. Keep going baby! Use this blueprint and the rest of the techniques in this book to manifest your true greatest self and the life you desire.

The Life of Your Dreams

What is the life of your dreams anyway? It's not usually something that falls into your lap all at once, like winning hundreds of millions of dollars in the lottery. Not saying that can't happen, it does; but the life of your dreams is a living, ever-evolving thing. You will always be adding to desires, looking to have more fun, finding inspiration in the new.

The moment one definitely commits oneself, then providence moves too. All sorts of things occur to help one that would never otherwise have occurred... Unforeseen incidents, meetings, and material assistance, which no man could have dreamed would have come his way.
   —J.W. Goethe

Make a decision to commit to your better life. You don't have to work hard at it. Your true nature is love, joy, and ease. This doesn't mean you won't ever have to do anything, but when you do act, you will be inspired to do so. Even if it is something that others term, *hard work*, it will excite you and your love of life.

You're on a planet of tremendous diversity. You won't always match up vibrationally with things around you. This doesn't make one right and another wrong, just different. As Shakespeare wrote so eloquently, *All the world's a stage, and all the men and women merely players*. Everyone is simply playing out their roles, yet underneath it all, you, me, all of us, we are pure love. Find that in others and you can't go wrong.

Enjoy the journey my friend because it is all a journey.

Peace out
Tashai J Lovington

WHAT'S YOUR STORY?

Do you have an interesting, funny, synchronistic, or other story or event that relates to the topics covered in this book?

Let me know!

Submit your story today for it to be considered for possible inclusion in future editions of this book.

Story guidelines:

Must relate to some process, tool or other from the book.

Must be a true story.

Send inquiries or story submissions here:
Tashai Arts LLC
6516 Monona Dr.
Suite 311
Monona, WI 53716
https://tashai.net

ACKNOWLEDGMENTS

Over the years, many have shared ideas, support or mentoring that has impacted my life, each in their own way. It's impossible to thank everyone and I apologize for anyone I have inadvertently not listed. Please know, that I do greatly appreciate you.

Special appreciation must go to: Joseph Campbell, Dr. Wayne Dyer, Louise Hay, Caroline Myss, Jack Canfield, Patty Aubery, Mike Dooley, Richard Bach, Esther and Jerry Hicks, Abraham Hicks, Darryl Anka and Bashar, James Redfield, Paramahansa Yogananda, Dr John Ryan, Shirley MacLaine, Ram Dass, The 14th Dalai Lama, Edgar Cayce, Kevin Todeschi, Denise Linn, Julia Cameron, James Malinchak, Nick and Megan Unsworth, Hal Elrod, Nick Ortner, and Brad Yates.

ABOUT THE AUTHOR

Tashai Lovington is a #1 bestselling author, course-creator, coach, speaker, filmmaker, and spiritual intuitive. She has appeared on public television and her work has been written up in numerous newspapers and periodicals. She was drawn to the study of new consciousness at a very early age which set her on a life-long adventure of discovery. Her work follows in the footsteps of some of the greatest teachers of leading-edge thought. She understands and implements the universal principle of attraction with deliberate intent in all areas of her life. Above all else, she has come to know that our natural state of being is one of joy and that the essence of life is to have fun.

For more of my books, courses, and art, visit my website:

https://tashai.net

facebook.com/tashai.lovington

twitter.com/tashailovington

instagram.com/tashai.lovington

tiktok.com/tashai.lov

ADDITIONAL RESOURCES

POPPING THE BUBBLE HOW TO CONNECT WITH YOU INNER GUIDANCE IN 7 DAYS OR LESS

HOME STUDY COURSE

To order go to : https://tashaiarts.samcart.com/products/
popping-the-bubble-workshop/

SPECIAL FREE BONUS GIFT FOR YOU

To help you achieve more success, there are FREE BONUS
RESOURCES for you at:

https://tashai.net